Heaven Time

*Discovering a New Way of Life After a
Near-Death Experience*

LORRI BREWER

Aquarius Publishing

Published in Canada by Aquarius Publishing

This title may be purchased in bulk for educational, business, fundraising, or sales promotional use through Aquarius Publishing. For more information please email sales@aquariuspublishing.com.

Author: Lorri Brewer
Editor: Amy VanVleck
Cover and Interior Design: Dean Pickup
Author Photo: Melissa Pickup

Printed in Canada by Friesens

Second Printing: May 2014

ISBN 978-0-9879519-0-8

Library and Archives Canada Cataloguing in Publication

Brewer, Lorri, 1968-
    Heaven time : discovering a new way of life after a near-death experience / Lorri Brewer.

Includes bibliographical references.
Issued also in electronic format.
ISBN 978-0-9879519-2-2 (bound).—ISBN 978-0-9879519-0-8 (pbk.)

    1. Near-death experiences—Case studies. 2. Near-death experiences—Religious aspects—Christianity. 3. Future life—Case studies. 4. Spiritual life—Case studies. 5. Heaven. 6. Brewer, Lorri, 1968-. I. Title.

BF1045.N4B649 2012   133.901'3   C2012-905031-8

Dedication

To the two most important men in my life, my husband Larry and my son A.J., who were my reasons for staying here and trying when I didn't know why. Without your love, patience, and encouragement this book would not have been possible.

To my mom Sarah who still teaches me something every day. I love you very much and I can't imagine my life without you, thank you for all of your prayers, support, and loving words of faith and encouragement.

And to my dad, my friend, you always had faith in me and in everything I did. Thank you for never leaving me, even though you are no longer here.

Lastly, to the thousands of near-death survivors who may silently struggle to comprehend their near-death experience and hide their voice for fear of ridicule and to those others who have had the courage to tell their story in spite of it...

This one is for you!

About the Author

LORRI BREWER is a daughter, sister, wife, mother and friend. She is also a successful business woman esteemed and appreciated by both her peers and clients for her strong moral compass, integrity, and professionalism. On September 19, 2010, Lorri crossed over from this  life to the afterlife and then returned with incredible knowledge and insight, which she now courageously shares with all of us in her book *Heaven Time*. Before being published, her amazing story and inspired reflections caught the attention of the CBC radio talk show *The Current*, with host Anna Maria Tremonti, the *International Association for Near-Death Studies* (IANDS), and the *Near Death Experience Research Foundation* (NDERF). Lorri has created a series of motivational lectures and workshops in which she shares her life-altering experience and encourages others to discover for themselves the meaning of life and death. When she's not working or writing, Lorri enjoys sharing a simple, quiet life with her husband Larry, her son A.J., and a treasured circle of friends and family in beautiful Edmonton, Alberta, Canada.

To contact Lorri for a speaking engagement or to learn more of her story, visit her website, www.lorribrewer.com, or email her publisher, Aquarius Publishing, at media@aquariuspublishing.com.

Acknowledgments

There are some things in life that just seem to happen to us, things that we don't have control over. It was never my intention to write a book, become an author, or have a near-death experience. All of that just seemed to happen to me.

But writing a book doesn't just happen, it seems to evolve. It takes a huge amount of time, patience, and effort from of a lot of great people. Although my name may be on the front cover and my thoughts are in the text, they certainly didn't get there without many other important contributors.

To my loving husband, Larry, who watched in horror as the life slipped from my body. Larry, you have witnessed the unimaginable and felt the fear and vulnerability of almost losing your new wife. And although that tragic night has left its scar on you, your love, faith, and devotion to me have never faltered. I love you with all my heart, and I thank you for loving me unconditionally and for protecting me when I forget how.

Through the privilege of parenting, my beautiful son, A.J., has taught me more about life than any other person I know. A.J., sweetheart, you have shown me the immense power a mother-and-son bond can have, and what unconditional love really means. Even though you have been forced to stare death in the face more times than any man your age, you have done so courageously, and you continue to choose to joyously embrace and celebrate life. You are my inspiration and you amaze me every day, I love you very much, and I am very proud of you and the man you have grown to be.

Like any parent with a child, my mom, Sarah, worries about me and loves me unconditionally. Mom, I am very blessed to have you still in my life. Your solid faith, your eighty years of wisdom and your unconditional love has seen me through many bleak and dark moments. The countless prayers you've said for me, so that I might find my way, have been answered and I am very happy to be sharing this accomplishment with you today. I love you, Mom.

And now to my Dream Team! Most people know that a manuscript cannot be called a book until the editor sculpts it into a masterpiece, the graphic designer paints, cleans, and polishes it, and the printer masterfully frames it perfectly so it can shine magnificently on display. Thank you to my Dream Team for taking my lump of coal, turning it into a diamond, polishing it so it glitters, and beautifully packaging it for all to see!

To my brilliant Editor, Amy Van Vleck at writewayedits.com, who was a major contributor to this project and had the hardest job of all. Spirituality is a very difficult topic to edit and very few can do it well. You masterfully balanced feeling my message as a reader, and then you skillfully simplified it, making my message much stronger and easier to understand. You have done what others have tried to do; where would this lump of coal be without you? Amy, I don't know how I can ever thank you for spinning my lump of coal into a diamond! It's amazing how our paths crossed and I feel very blessed to not only call you my brilliant editor but now also my friend. You are a true gem, with all my heart, thank you!

To my incredible Designer, Dean Pickup at dpict Visual Communications thanks for polishing my work! Your passion to create is evident in your award-winning book covers and beautiful technical artistry in layout design. From our first conversation, I loved your enthusiasm and dedication to your profession, and happily relinquished complete creative control to you. There is so much more that goes into the detailed layout and design than I could have ever imagined. Thank you for beautifully polishing my diamond and for your incredible integrity, compassion, and dedication. It boggles my mind that you can create such an eloquent simple cover that can describe so much. You are a wonderfully gifted and talented artist. Great job, Dean!

To the wonderful team at Friesen's Printing, who has masterfully bundled, bound, and packaged my work for all to see: thank you for the quotes, printing, the binding, the packaging, and the shipping. Also, I am very thankful to Aquarius Publishing for co-ordinating the whole process, teaching me about author marketing and PR campaigns, and for distributing this book.

Lastly, I am eternally grateful to my long-time friend and cardiologist, Dr. Gulamhuseien. Throughout my life I have endured more than 120 SVT attacks and suffered through more than twenty cardioversions. Doctor G., we have known each other for seventeen years, and together, we've struggled through three of my failed heart ablation procedures and I feel so blessed that you agreed to do the fourth procedure. I guess the fourth time was the charm! Thank you for curing my arrhythmia, and my eternal thanks for giving me a chance to live life! I will always consider you the best cardiologist and friend. Thank you for not giving up on me when so many others did. Thank you for changing my life!

I need to thank the nursing staff who listened to me without judgment on the night of my near-death experience. You shared your knowledge and gave me guidance to seek further information from experts who specialize in near-death experiences. This made a huge difference in my search for answers and recovery process.

I am forever grateful to all the devoted members at the International Association for Near-Death Studies (www.IANDS.com), and to Dr. Jeffrey Long and his staff at the Near Death Experience Research Foundation (www.NDERF.com). To my incredible extended family, Uncle Ken and Aunt Marg Booker: thank you for supporting Larry when he needed it most. I am also grateful to my wonderful friends, Karen Mandrusiak, Susan Davis, and Veronica Mulder who always showed me such respect, compassion, and love and reminded me often that I am indeed normal!

Thank you all!
Always my best,
Lorri

Table of Contents

PART THREE – Celebrating Life

Preface

*S*piritual awakening and spiritual intuitiveness can be easily attained by anyone searching for them, but they are much more difficult to explain. Surprisingly, a spiritual awakening is such a simple process! But that which is simple can be made difficult. This book is committed to teaching that process in a simple and easy-to-understand manner. It is a combination of a *how-to book* and *feel things out for yourself* book!

There is no right or wrong way, there is only *your* way; and I am very honoured to be a part of your journey. My real journey began after my near-death experience. It has been reported by the Near Death Experience Research Foundation that around 750 people a day in the United States have a near-death experience! Near-death experiences are really quite common, but what is *not* commonly discussed is the recovery process. It's generally assumed that anyone who has survived a near-death trauma, experienced a little piece of Heaven, touched the love of a deceased family member(s), and who has come back from the dead is grateful, ecstatic, and filled with divine purpose. But that isn't always the case.

Some near-death survivors have written about their experience, but large portions do not, and that is because the after-effects and the recovery process can be very difficult and incredibly painful. I was a survivor that was *not* happy to be back. This book is based on my intensely painful journey and the detailed journal entries that assisted me in my recovery process. But it is through the actual experience of my near-death trauma and survival of its after-effects that I attained—and have retained—a heightened level of spiritual intuitiveness and ever-present connectivity to a Higher Power that allows me to share with you what I *now* know.

Heaven Time will entice your curiosity about near-death experiences, and it will examine and compare the different viewpoints of science, religion, and spirituality. It will help you evaluate your *current perception* regarding your purpose in this life, and it will provide a step-by-step, simple exercise guide to show you how to live in the *here and now*, increase your spiritual intuitiveness, discover what your true, authentic purpose in this life is, and connect with *your* Higher Power. This book will answer your questions and calm any fears that you may have about death and dying. It will help you better understand and relate to a loved one who may be actively dying this very minute. It will help near-death survivors and their families, who are struggling with the after-effects of a near-death experience, learn how to cope with their new changes.

So who would benefit from this book? Everyone! Because happiness is contagious—and so is misery. Just as "You are what you eat," you are a mirror to the company you keep. We are all individually connected to one Divine Source, therefore making us all essentially one. It is in being connected to Oneness that we are collectively only as strong as our weakest vibration. If the weakest vibration were powerful and strong, just imagine what our world would be like! Imagine what our lives would be like!

It wasn't long ago that I was the weakest vibration. One of the most important reasons for my putting these words to paper is very simple. It is to find and celebrate others with the weakest vibration and help raise their *vibrational level*, which in turn will strengthen us all.

After reading this book, through recognition and acceptance you will have reached a superior level of spiritual *connectiveness* to a Higher Power, whether conceived as Divine Source, God, Universe, Source Energy, and/or Creator. It is through Oneness that you will have an increased level of psychic intuitiveness, and you will have found a purposeful direction for this lifetime that will lead you to financial prosperity, health, and ineffable happiness.

With the knowledge of my near-death experience, and my understanding and documenting my recovery process, I have been granted the joy of living in everlasting connectivity to a Higher Power and living in a heightened state of awareness. It is with delight that I present this book to you. These words will not only touch you but will positively influence your thoughts and actions.

Thank you for joining me on this journey. Trust that you are exactly where you are meant to be at this very moment. May the solace that you seek be found divinely and perfectly within. May all that you share be done with graciousness, and all that you learn be received for your highest good. May your own private, spiritual journey be filled with love, peace, and joy.

With Love and Blessings,

Lorri

Introduction

*T*he words *near-death experience* (NDE) never had any meaning for me. Why would they? I had never researched the topic, nor did I find it particularly interesting. In fact, I had never believed in the phenomenon at all. I thought it involved a chemical imbalance in the brain or else was simply a matter of someone seeking attention.

On the night I died, September 19, 2010, I knew that something very profound had happened to me. It was the first time those three little words became very comforting and horrifyingly scary at the same time. When I heard the nurse say *near-death experience,* I didn't know what that really meant, but I was comforted knowing that the changes I felt within my body had a name. Although I didn't know anything about *near-death experiences* or their *after-effects*, the thought that these unwanted foreign changes would never leave scared the hell out of me.

For almost a year, I hoped that I would return to *normal.* But it soon became apparent that there was no such thing as *normal.* Battling severe depression and suicidal thoughts, suppressing unspeakable fear and becoming reclusive, I launched an obsessive pursuit for answers in order to get some relief from my excruciating emotional pain. My relief came in a paradigm shift—a shift in my thinking, my perception, and my behaviour. All my previous journal writings had unknowingly explored and deciphered a universal search process and recovery plan that I am now going to share with you. It was in accepting and following this process that I found a heightened state of consciousness which allows constant connection to a Divine Source. This state of *being* is also available to you should you decide to follow the same process.

Being tapped into a permanent connection to the Divine Source allowed me to learn lessons and receive profound explanations. This exchange of information comes to me in the form of spiritual teachings, coming from spiritual teachers. I am able to access several teachers. Depending on the topics or situations that I seek knowledge about, these spiritual teachers individually or collectively offer wisdom, strength, courage, patience, understanding, and/or clarity. I call these wise teachers my Choir.

I've labelled them my Choir because, although they may offer teachings as individuals, they are essentially the representation of Oneness or a collective unity of One. They are filled with unfathomable wisdom beyond my human capacity for expansion, creation, or imagination. My Choir has provided incredible explanations and profound insights into many controversial questions about which I was curious. The wisdom, love, understanding, and knowledge that I've received from my Choir are too powerful and exhilarating to keep to myself.

It is so thrilling, even today, to be reminded of the *gift* that my Choir is. There are some days when it feels as if they have been with me my whole life. By the time of publication, it will be nearly two years since I found them! I access their infinite wisdom constantly throughout the day; most of the time I don't even realize I am doing it. It's ironic that for so long I was terribly frightened when I could hear them. I fought desperately to deny the thought of their possible existence, and the thought of opening that *paranormal* door gripped me with paralyzing fear. Now, I can't imagine life without my Choir!

As you read, you will clearly see and enjoy the difference between my writing style and that of my Choir. When *I* am speaking, it is in the present tense, even though I might be describing something that happened in the past. However, my Choir tends to be in third person, past tense, depending on the topic. Any dialogue from my Choir will be clearly marked, as I will not take any credit for their work. The privilege I receive is putting pen to paper.

Heaven Time is written from a highly spiritual point of view. However, being born and raised Catholic, I admit that I am part skeptic, so this book floats between three viewpoints: Religion, Science, and Spirituality. Since surviving a near-death experience, being raised in the Catholic faith, finding higher consciousness through spirituality, and scientifically trying to make sense of it all, I share my personal beliefs with respect to all three viewpoints. After all, we are multi-dimensional, and it would be remiss of me to try to focus on only one dimension.

The creation and development of this book was not intended to convince anyone of the existence of an afterlife, prove that near-death experiences are real, or change any religious beliefs. *Heaven Time* is based solely on my personal beliefs since recovering from an NDE and enjoying another dimension on this physical plane. Some of the diverse topics that I will be discussing with you, based on what I've learned from living with my Choir, are death, dying, living, spirits, angels, karma, abortion, Heaven, Hell, and the end of the world! My insights on such topics may or may not match what science says, or what the Bible says, or what the universal laws have to say. I am ecstatically happy to share my views with you, but please remember that *Heaven Time* is based on *my* personal beliefs and is not intended to offend anyone.

My Choir says that spiritual intuitiveness and awakening are attained easily by anyone who is passionately and actively searching for them, because their minds are already open to change and new opportunities. But it is much more difficult to explain, and I couldn't imagine this undertaking without the help of my Choir. It's important to understand that because the teacher showed up doesn't mean the student did! To be successful in this quest, you must *want* to make changes and be prepared to put in some effort.

Heaven Time is a combination of an *easy-to-read*, compelling story of a near-death experience and a *how-to* book with a step-by-step guide consisting of simple exercises to show you how to evaluate your current life's purpose, live in the *here and now*, increase your spiritual intuitiveness and connect with your Higher Power. Lastly, it is a motivational and inspirational book that will answer your questions and calm any fears that you may have about death and dying. It will inspire hope in other near-death survivors and their families who struggle with the after-effects that a near-death trauma might bring. I hope my readers will appreciate that my intentions in writing this book have been to tantalize the mind, stimulate the heart's emotion, strengthen the foundations of faith, and inspire personal hope.

When creating and developing *Heaven Time*, it was important to me to achieve three writing goals. The first goal was to be so brutally, hard-core honest that any reader could feel my pain and anguish, and subsequently, my sense of peace, elation, and love. Secondly, to provide very detailed examples and simple analogies so all readers could follow the simple step-by-step guides. Thirdly, to pen as precisely as possible the translated version of my Choir's intentions so each reader could maximize his or her experience.

Heaven Time has four main sections. Besides a Glossary, the main written portion is separated into three parts. Part One is called "The Journey," and it introduces the emotional, intimate story of my personal struggle with a near-death experience and shares important personal views. This intense account of a near-death trauma will not only ignite the reader's curiosity about death, dying, and the afterlife, but will also allow the reader to share a roller coaster of emotions. This part also outlines the excruciating pain of struggling to cope with the life-altering after-effects of a near-death experience. Part One is not only the foundation for Part Two but also serves as an example throughout the second part to illustrate important teachings and learning lessons.

Part Two, "The Shift," describes a successful search process that will benefit everyone who is searching for answers. It does not pertain to any particular struggle or pain. Pain is universal, and struggle is too! It is through *feeling* that you will now begin to experience and understand important teachings. The need to rationalize or use logic will also be satisfied here. By enjoying a gentle *how-to* guide, you will get to decide what actions *you* must take to find the answers *you* seek. It is in this part that the lessons will require some practice and a little patience.

Part Three, the last of the three central sections, is called "Celebrating Life." It celebrates the epiphanies you've had and all the lessons that you have learned thus far. The recovery process doesn't *have* to be painful; we choose whether it will be painful or not. The choices we make dictate whether recovery will be easy or hard. What will you choose? You have nothing to lose and everything to gain. So, if you're questioning life's meaning, have lost your identity, have suffered a loss, or wonder what your purpose is, then I would be honoured if you would join me on this journey. You will be glad you did!

When learning a new lesson or being taught a new concept, it can be frustrating if you can't seem to catch on right away. Learning a new concept is done with your mind, using your powers of logic. Finding spiritual awakening or spiritual awareness requires not only *logic* but also *feeling*. It is unrealistic to think that learning a math equation or learning how to cook is the same type of learning as anything spiritual. That is why *Heaven Time* is separated into three specific parts. In Part One you get to *feel*, using your emotions and very little logic or thought. Part Two employs your mind and logic, using your emotions as a gauge. Part Three celebrates intuition and expands upon your newfound spiritual awareness.

In Part Two you will notice some repetition. I use the technique of *re-capping*. I do this so that readers won't have to constantly flip to the back of the book to look up the word in a glossary, only to lose their reading momentum. I have tried to keep the recapping to no more than three times per concept, as anything more than that can be disruptive.

It is my hope that while reading *Heaven Time* you will feel my pain and then celebrate my joy. It is while sharing my journey that you will begin to experience your own spiritual awakening. I do not believe in the old saying, *Do as I say, not as I do*; but, I wholeheartedly believe, *Feel what I felt, be as I feel.*

Epiphanies are not taught; they are stumbled upon and felt. The answers that you seek are found in exactly the same way, perfectly within. So let's get started. We have a lot of ground to cover. Remember, it's not about *thinking*, it's about *feeling*. Now relax, sit back, and enjoy *your* journey!

1

The Journey

CHAPTER ONE

In the Beginning

*The longest journey begins
with a single step.*

~Patañjali

ow is it that I have come here today, writing these words? When did this journey of mine really begin? I guess if I'm being totally honest with you, my journey started in adolescence. I was sixteen and had just started high school. I had a part-time job at a local department store and was working at least four six-hour evening shifts a week. My life was so hectic; I was going to school full-time and had a full course load. The homework assignments were heavy and nothing like I was used to. On the evenings that I worked, it would be close to eleven o'clock by the time I got home. Then, tired or not, I would still have to do a couple of hours of homework. It was caffeine pills that kept me awake and kept me going during these long hours.

I had just started dating my high school sweetheart. Although I had dated other boys, I knew this one was special. We had a deeper connection than a mere high school crush. As a young woman, I truly believed the connection we shared is what others would call *love*. For the first time in my life I experienced a host of emotions very foreign to me. I learned about jealousy when he would flirt with other girls, or I would feel sadness when he would rather spend time with his buddies. But he also showed me what it felt like to be valued. He valued my intelligence, my personality, and my sense of humour. I felt a sense of grounding and security when we were together. Every time I saw him my heart would pound and my stomach would churn—which now sounds more like the stomach flu than love!

With the pressures of school and the long shifts of my part-time job, not to mention the emotional roller coaster of this new relationship, stressors were bombarding my every waking hour. I began making choices that weren't very smart or healthy for a growing and maturing body. I continued to supplement my diet with caffeine pills, and ate chocolate bars for quick energy. I used appetite suppressants and took laxatives to keep me looking lean and slender.

As if all this wasn't enough, I had shot up to an alarming five-feet-ten–inches tall. I was one of the tallest girls in my classes and was very self-conscious about it. I was physically active and not overweight, but as with most teenage girls, even perfection wouldn't have been good enough.

On a beautiful warm day late in the fall, I was happy to be heading home from school and not off to my part-time job. I was looking forward to the night off and getting some much-needed rest. I had skipped my last class and spent the afternoon with my boyfriend. Life was perfect. Everything was perfect.

As three-thirty approached, I began panicking. I needed to catch the usual bus home so my mom wouldn't be suspicious that I had missed school. As I ran up a flight of stairs to catch my bus, I felt a sharp, stabbing pain in the left side of my neck. Along with the pain, I could feel a horrible fluttering in my neck like the wings of a hummingbird panicking to get out.

My mouth went dry, my heart was pounding, my head was throbbing, and my left arm was tingling as if it had fallen asleep. I had no idea what was happening to me. I desperately tried to calm myself. This must be a panic attack, I thought. I scolded myself for working too many long hours, not getting enough sleep, panicking about skipping school, taking too many caffeine pills, and having a poor diet.

By the time I got home I was exhausted. As I lay down on my bed, my heart was pounding so hard and fast that my headboard was actually moving against the wall with each beat. My mom was concerned that my demanding schedule was too overwhelming for someone my age. She gave me a couple of aspirin and I fell into a deep sleep. Several hours later I awoke feeling much better. My heart was no longer fluttering and the pain was gone. I vowed to work fewer hours and quit the caffeine pills and appetite suppressants.

My second attack occurred when I was nineteen. I knew instinctively that something was really wrong and that I needed immediate medical attention. After being rushed by ambulance to the hospital and undergoing a multitude of tests, I was eventually diagnosed with the cardiac condition known as Supraventricular Tachycardia, or SVT. An intravenous (IV) line was put into my arm. Strong medicines were administered to stop my heart momentarily so that it could reset or convert itself into a normal rhythm. Little did I know that my next twenty-five years would be riddled with SVTs!

An SVT is a rapid, irregular heartbeat, or arrhythmia. During an SVT, the heart doesn't pump, it quivers. With medical intervention, the heart is stopped; it converts, then begins to beat normally again. In the majority of SVT events, the heart converts without any complications. However, on rare occasions, an SVT can be fatal.

After each attack, I spend approximately three to six hours in the hospital depending on the severity. A medical team monitors my vital signs continuously, ensuring that another episode will not occur. For a day or two after each attack I am left totally exhausted. My body feels battered and I ache everywhere. My heart is *irritable*, with uncomfortable, spontaneous, irregular flutters.

I am lucky that, for the most part, I have been able to live a relatively normal life. Although I never married my high school sweetheart, I did get married, and was blessed to be able to conceive, carry, and deliver my only child, a beautiful son. During my pregnancy, I constantly worried about having an SVT attack. The administration of strong drugs was a concern for my baby's health. I did have one SVT episode, which thankfully converted naturally on my way to the hospital so that no drugs had to be administered.

When my son was two years old, my husband's job relocated us to a remote northern town. As I entered this godforsaken ghost town, the sign on the highway claimed that the population was twelve hundred, which must have also included some deer, elk, and bears! The only inhabitants of this town were the employees who worked at the local plant, a couple of Royal Canadian Mounted Police (RCMP) officers, one doctor, and a handful of nurses.

We were staying in company housing, which turned out to be a small mobile home in a beaten-down mobile home park. We moved there in November. The snow was chest high, and the temperatures were so frigid that human flesh would freeze in seconds. For the next four months, until spring came, I was stranded in this trashy mobile home park in the middle of nowhere, locked away by freezing temperatures with almost no human contact. My husband worked long hours. He would leave before I awoke and arrive home a couple of hours before bed. The isolation was emotionally devastating for a relatively new wife and mother. I missed home, which was more than three hours away.

As spring blossomed, the other housebound mothers and children began to emerge. My son and I started making new friends. We joined a Mom and Tots group to help pass the long, miserable days. The only thing I looked forward to was travelling back home twice a month and staying the weekend to replenish our grocery supply. Most importantly,

I loved reconnecting with my family, whom I missed terribly. Then, as the weekend and the family visits and frantic grocery shopping were all coming to an end, the realization that we were headed back to the bleak isolation began to panic me. I hated that place and its dank, hollow existence. I hated my husband for moving us there, but most of all I hated that he was happy and didn't seem to care that I was miserable. He had a job that paid good money and nothing else seemed to matter.

As the hour of departure grew closer and closer, I was frantic. Truth be told, I began panicking and obsessively worrying about returning to that hellhole the moment we got into the city. The entire weekend was a constant reminder that we had to go back. Then a couple of hours before we would have to leave—surprise, surprise—I would have an SVT!

Much to the dismay of my husband, an SVT was a nuisance with respect to getting back to the hellhole before dark. Nevertheless, I would be converted at the hospital then released and on my way back to the hellhole once again. The incessant disgust and hatred I felt made my SVT episodes even more frequent.

Upon departure from the city that I loved and called home, an SVT began to appear almost like clockwork. This led my husband to understandably believe that the weekend city visits were too stressful for me. Our grocery shopping trips were now cut down to day trips only.

My marriage began to fall apart. I began to question what my purpose was. The guilt associated with my sense of obligation and responsibility to my son, to keep our family together, began to fester. Now deprived of weekend family visits, I was exposed to stressful one-day shopping trips. We had to leave very early, travel three hours into the city, shop like crazy, then drive another three hours back before dark.

My anger, resentment, and guilt were boiling over. My lack of independent financial resources and my fear of changing my situation left me frustrated and exhausted. The hopelessness was getting too hard to hide. Then, my worst fear came true. My nightmare materialized into reality and there was nothing I could do about it.

CHAPTER TWO

My
Worst Fear

A life lived in fear
is a life half lived.

~Spanish proverb

Most of my SVTs happened in the city, which had incredible doctors, state of the art equipment, and fully functioning hospitals. I had always taken for granted that when you see a hospital, you will be greeted with competent doctors and state of the art equipment. I was wrong: not in that hellhole. The doctor was a general practitioner and did not have much emergency room trauma experience. Most of the emergencies were airlifted to the nearest city hospital; and the average age of his patients was around twenty-five, and they were therefore probably pretty healthy!

One night when my son was three years old, I had just put him to bed when I had another SVT episode. We took my son to our neighbour's home so my husband could take me to the hellhole hospital. The nurses had just completed training in ALS, which stands for Advanced Life Support, which means they know how to use the defibrillator! Normally, in a city hospital, I am converted within twenty minutes and left to recover for a couple of hours. Normally, doctors are on site and know what to do immediately, but unfortunately for me, this was not the case.

The doctor was at home eating his dinner, as he had just left the hospital for the night. When he finished eating his dinner he finally graced me with his presence—one hour later! He asked what medicine I wanted, to which I responded *Verapamil*. I told him that was what the city hospitals gave me and I responded very well to it. Due to his inexperience and his assessment of how I was presenting, he refused to give me that medicine. He tried another drug called *Adenosine*. Both of these drugs are designed to momentarily stop your heart and convert it to start up normally again. By this time I had been in the hellhole hospital for four hours and no one had a clue what to do with me!

He called the city hospital, from where he was getting direction over the phone. The city hospital told him that because I had been in this condition for so long, the best and immediate option would be to cardiovert. This means that they stick one large pad on your chest just off to the left and the other large pad on your back between your shoulder blades. The pads have wires in them so that when they send the electric shock it is specifically directed to the heart. This ensures that the patient receives the current –and not a healthcare worker!

I started to cry. It wasn't fair; because this idiot we call *a doctor* had to finish his supper, and because he didn't know what to do, I now had to pay for his ignorance! I was very upset and sobbing; I didn't understand what was happening to me. When I asked one of the nurses if she could hold my hand, she laughed and said, "No way, I'm not getting shocked." Realizing her insensitivity, she covered it up by saying, "No one will be holding your hand, we just can't do that." Because the nursing staff had just finished taking a course on using the defibrillator they all seemed pretty excited to see it in action ... and I was their guinea pig!

The doctor promised me that he would give me something so that I wouldn't feel it or even remember it. I begged him to *knock me out*.

"Don't worry, you won't feel a thing," he reassured me. They put some sleepy medicine into my intravenous tube and waited a few minutes. I was still talking and I told them that I wasn't sleeping yet, that I was still awake. I heard the machine start to hum a soft squeal then get louder and louder. No one was near my bed. Then, out of nowhere, it felt like a large size 14 shoe kicked me on my breastbone and bounced me off a concrete wall. I could hear myself involuntarily let out a shrilling scream that seemed to knock my air out.

As soon as the kick was over, I sobbed uncontrollably because I understood that the 'kick' meant I was being *cardioverted* and that the doctor had lied: I felt everything. I was horrified to realize that my SVT wasn't gone and that the excruciating pain of cardioversion hadn't worked. Unimaginable fear rushed over me when I realized that he was going to do it to me again—and there was nothing I could do about it! I was at this blundering doctor's mercy.

By this time I'd been in my SVT episode for almost six hours, which is totally unheard of. When the heart is in SVT it is not pumping or effectively moving blood around in the body. The heart is actively quivering and pounding hard; the heart is a muscle. If the heart muscle quivers and pounds for too long it will get tired. If it gets too tired it could just stop—and I would be dead! No one really knows how long the heart muscle can quiver and pound like that. Believe me, I've asked! It seems the younger and healthier you are, most likely the longer it can quiver, but still, youth is no guarantee. So that is why when I go the hospital and tell them that I am having an SVT, they frantically rush to get it converted as soon as possible. That is why SVTs can be potentially fatal.

I desperately prayed to God that this horrific ordeal would soon be over and that I would never see this idiot we called *doctor* again. But it wasn't over; I was on my way to a second shock attempt.

This time, even though he gave me a little more milky white medicine, I was still awake with a blurred understanding of what was happening. A part of me seemed more dulled. I could hear the machine start off with a soft, squealing hum, then get louder and louder. You cannot predict when the kick will come. Then, again without warning, it felt as if I'd fallen from the top branch of a tree and had my air knocked out. As I gasped to catch my breath, I realized to my relief that I was no longer in SVT.

As I was slowly recovering, the doctor came to my bedside and said, "None of this would have happened this way if you would have had a medical protocol from your cardiologist." Amazing! This blundering boob couldn't get it right, and now this horrible ordeal and traumatic conversion process was *my* fault.

After that, when any medical team anywhere treated my SVT and suggested cardioversion, I aggressively and flatly refused. They would insist that I would not feel it and that it was very effective in converting SVT, but the doctor from hell showed me that what they said was not to be trusted … ever again.

Shortly after that ordeal, my husband moved us to another small town much closer to the city and to my family. My son was around four years old when my husband and I bought our first home together with the hopes and dreams of finally settling down. By this time my SVTs were happening very frequently, sometimes weekly. My husband was still working long hours and was now actively involved in the community as volunteer firefighter. I became a real estate agent, which took me away most evenings once my son went to bed. My husband and I were no longer spending much time together and with my frequent SVT episodes, I began taking myself to the hospital.

When I would be having an SVT episode, I would put my son in his booster chair with some toys and drive to the hospital, acting as if nothing was wrong, hoping not to alarm my small child. By now the hospital's staff was very familiar with me. They would escort me to a small emergency room bay, where I would lay in a semi-sitting position on the bed. My son would sit on the bed with me and I would put his back to my chest so he couldn't see what was going on.

I would begin to read to him while they put an intravenous tube into my arm to administer the drug. I would get my son to turn the pages so he would be preoccupied with the story and turning the pages and not with the drama of an SVT. As they administered the drug, I would momentarily lose my breath and have to stop reading. The effectiveness of the drug would allow my heart to convert. I would then catch my breath and continue reading and playing with him until I was released.

On a couple of occasions when the drug didn't work, the nurses took my son from me and brought him to the waiting area, where they would show him *new toys*, while the trauma staff worked on converting me. My son and I experienced more than twenty of these trips while he was young and easy to preoccupy; thankfully, he has little memory of any of them.

Just before my son's seventh birthday, my husband and I separated and later divorced. My son and I moved away to a larger center, closer to family. I continued with my real estate career and began a new life as a single mom. Although it could be challenging at times juggling the demands of commission sales, raising a son, and running a household, it was also very rewarding. But, for sure, one fact remained: my SVTs kept happening.

An SVT can happen day or night, awake or asleep, when working or enjoying a vacation. It can happen when you least expect it. There is no way to control it. Now, being single, the spontaneity and unpredictability of the SVTs added yet another huge level of fear and uncertainty to my already shaky life.

* * *

CHAPTER THREE

I Am My Own Worst Enemy

Manifestation is showing a presence—
when conditions are sufficient,
something manifests itself.
~Thich Nhat Hanh

*I*n March 2005, my niece was an RCMP member when one of her troop mates was murdered in the Mayerthorpe, Alberta, RCMP killings. He was one of four who was senselessly gunned down. Our country was devastated. It was impossible to reason or even comprehend how this tragedy could have happened. When we hear of any service personnel losing their life while protecting their fellow citizens, we can't help but take a quick moment to feel some remorse, even if we didn't know them personally.

For days, the news coverage constantly bombarded us with horrible pictures, we listened to terribly sad interviews with grieving family members, and the public's angry demand for justice mounted. My niece asked me to go with her to her troop mate's funeral. I was honoured to be there for her in this terribly sad time. There is only an approximate ten-year difference in age between my niece and me, so we related to each other more like sisters. I loved her dearly and wanted so much to take this pain from her. As the funeral date loomed, so did my anxiety.

On the day of the funeral, I met with my niece, who still needed to get changed into her dress uniform. I quietly watched as she got ready. I couldn't help but dwell on the fact that this could have been her. Even though I passionately understood her desire to be in law enforcement and respected her decision, my overwhelming fear of losing her sickened me.

When she finished dressing, we drove together to the church where the funeral ceremony was being held. As we neared the church, my emotions and anxiety were peaking. I was triggered with such sadness remembering *my own* dear friend, also an RCMP member, who had been killed in a car accident only a few years earlier.

When we arrived at the church, all you could see were hundreds of RCMP members in their Red Serge dress uniforms. The day was cloudy and overcast. It was not quite spring yet, nothing was blooming, and everything was still brown. The ground was cold and the day was chilly. I parked the vehicle and we proceeded into the church, stopping to sign the memorial book.

My thoughts were racing. My anger began to boil with thoughts that human life seemed to have no value. The unfathomable sadness and grief that plagued this day hung in the air. The church was hot and stuffy, almost suffocating. The sad truth that this young RCMP member lost his life while keeping us safe, and the frustration and anger at the fact that this tragedy could have possibly been prevented, also seemed to linger.

Seeing the late RCMP member's pregnant wife, who was expecting their second child, was devastating for me. The culmination of hearing the pipers tuning their instruments, looking at a sea of hundreds of Red Serge uniforms, and hearing others cry as they reunited, was more than I could bear. I gasped for air . . . then it happened . . . I was having an SVT...

I started to panic. How was I going to sneak away? Where is the hospital in this town? What do I do? This is such an important day! How can this happen now? Why today?

As I had this panicked look on my face, my niece touched my arm, "Are you okay?" I tried to reassure her, but she is a cop, and you're not likely to put one over on her.

"Yes, of course, I'm just hot and it's stuffy in here. I'll be right back. I'm going to get a glass of water." Because the day was chilly and overcast, I was wearing a turtleneck sweater, which made the matter worse. I began to sweat profusely.

The church had a little kitchen, where I went to get a much-needed drink of water; it also provided me a few seconds to figure out my game plan. If I could last six hours in an SVT in that hellhole of a hospital with a blundering doctor, I decided I could get through this one-hour funeral.

I took two very strong beta blockers, thinking this would help my situation, then after the service I would go to the hospital. (A beta blocker is a type of drug that slows down the heart and blocks substances like adrenaline when present in the system.) I could hear the music in the church playing now; the service was about to begin. I quickly made my way back to my seat. My niece sat to my left and her friend sat to my right. I tried not to touch my niece in any way for fear she would feel my pounding, racing heart.

As I inched farther away from my niece, I pushed closer to her friend who was on my other side. The service began, the church was hot, my turtleneck was suffocating me, and my screaming internal panic didn't allow me to hear or understand any words of the service.

How long could I last? *Could* I drop dead? Am I *doing* the right thing? Will my niece be angry with me? What happens if she finds out…? Then a quiet whisper in my right ear came from my niece's friend: "Are you all right?"

"Yes, thank you, I'm fine. Why?" I asked as if nothing was wrong.

"Well, I'm a paramedic, and I can feel your heart pounding; that could be very serious. Would you mind if I take your pulse?"

Great! How wonderful! Squished over in the pew and now in the clutches of a freakin' paramedic ... just my luck! *Now* what am I supposed to do? When my body is in an SVT it is very difficult to take a pulse in my wrist. Because she had no real idea what was going on, I conceded, hoping she would *think* she felt one and would leave me alone.

Of course, I was surrounded by cops, and a certain observant one to my left wanted to know what we were doing. "Nothing," I whispered. "*Why* is she taking your pulse, then?" my niece questioned.

Miss Paramedic pipes in, "I can't seem to get a pulse." Damn! *Busted*! Now what am I supposed to do? How the hell am I getting out of this one? So I decided I had only one option left, and that was to pull out the *Auntie card*. (This is an imaginary card that says that you are wiser and smarter; she is younger and is going to listen to her aunt now!)

However, this niece had an imaginary card of her own, and she used it. It is called the *cop card*! She was the boss, and *I* was going to listen to *her* now! So while the funeral of her troop mate was in session, the pews jam-packed, leaving absolutely no room for privacy, we sat debating whether or not she was taking me to the hospital. She then began to lose her composure, her eyes filled with tears; she told me that she'd lost this troop mate and wasn't prepared to lose another. I began to cry.

She sacrificed saying her final farewell to her friend to take me to the hospital for a stupid SVT, which seem so trivial compared to the reason for which we had gathered. I was riddled with guilt, frustration, anger, sadness, and helplessness. I apologized profusely, but it didn't change the situation or make the matter any better ... nor did it make me feel better; I felt horrible.

Once we arrived at the hospital, the presence of my niece's uniform commanded attention. We were quickly ushered into an emergency bay, where they promptly began working on me. By this time we were both crying and holding hands. This was a small community where everyone knew that the fallen member's funeral service was that day, and her being in a dress uniform prompted even more attention and gossip.

Unfortunately, when I came to the initial conclusion that I would stay at the funeral, I'd made a horrible mistake by taking two, slow-releasing, strong beta blockers, which apparently now prevented the doctors from medically converting me. They tried everything. They called my cardiologist for some much-needed advice as I was adamantly and aggressively refusing to be shocked with cardioversion. By this time my niece and I had both forgotten about the funeral, as this matter had quickly become much more serious.

The attending doctor was awesome—very patient, caring, and understanding. It also helped that his every move was being scrutinized by an overprotective RCMP member who was not about to take crap from anyone! The deal he made with me was that I would receive a larger than normal dosage of medicine to stop my heart. If that didn't work he would have no alternative but to use cardioversion. It was the only way. I reluctantly agreed and understood the seriousness of the situation.

He prepared the dosage and started putting the medicine into my IV line. As the medicine was hitting my bloodstream, I could feel it go up my arm. I would lose track of this sensation before my shoulder and just around my armpit. As I felt the medicine going in, I could feel my niece gently stroking my arm in such a loving and tender manner.

Then everything went black. I could feel nothing. I could hear nothing. It was just total darkness. I had no thoughts. It felt as if hours had passed when I was startled awake to my niece's screaming sob. Her continued loving touch softly caressing my arm resumed and was now registering in my mind.

Apparently, once the medicine was administered my heart stopped and flatlined for several seconds. I didn't see any angels or Heaven's door; I really didn't give it much thought. I was just grateful my SVT was gone. To this day I feel horrible that *I* caused her to miss saying goodbye to her friend. For a long time I had horrible guilt from taking those two powerful pills which resulted in a very traumatic experience.

This will remain a very profound experience for the two of us, and one that we will share and always remember for the rest of our lives. The blessing of this unwanted heart condition is what brings me to writing and sharing it with you today—a near-death experience and recovery. Without this curse, I wouldn't have touched paradise; without its pain, I wouldn't have touched peace. It is a dominant reminder in my life that *time* is very precious and that *life* is very fragile.

After this particular episode, and in hindsight, I learned about the triggers that activate an SVT and I quickly became more proactive, not reactive, toward this condition. Although an SVT episode can be spontaneous and scary, I am sure that you can see the predictable warning signals that I clearly missed throughout most of my life, causing me to have more than 120 of these attacks! The emotionally painful part of my condition is how these SVT episodes have affected not only me, but also the other people in my life. Once I understood the predictability of an SVT, I no longer was unprepared or fearful ... until *that night*... the night of my NDE.

There was *nothing* and *no one* to prepare me for *that night*. There were no triggers, no warning signals, no stress ... and no obvious reason for it to have happened.

* * *

CHAPTER FOUR

My Anchor

Somebody should tell us, right at the start of our lives, that we are dying.
Then we might live life to the limit, every minute of every day.
Do it! I say. Whatever you want to do, do it now!
There are only so many tomorrows.

~Pope Paul VI, 1897–1978

For many years after my divorce, I was a single working mom. Although I loved my job as a real estate agent, the demands and pressures of commission sales took their toll on me. But two factors remained forever consistent in my life: my endless love for my son and my plaguing SVTs.

My son meant the world to me, and he was all that I ever had. He was my inspiration, my joy, and the reason I got up each and every day. Through the years as my son grew, he watched me suffer through many SVT attacks, which at times were difficult for him to endure. There is something to say about the magical, unbreakable bond between a mother and a child. As I was a single mom, this already unbreakable bond that we shared was amplified after each SVT that we endured together.

Because we considered my SVT events as a part of who I am, they became a normal part of our lives. We didn't really take them too seriously;

my outcomes were always positive, and my heart always converted. At times these attacks seemed more like a nuisance than a threat.

When my son was thirteen, I met a wonderful man who showed me unconditional love and patience every day. I didn't want to tell my future husband that I suffered from a serious heart arrhythmia that would frequently send me to the hospital. Meeting and sharing my life with him significantly lowered my stress levels. I feared his rejection. I had always been very outgoing, free-spirited, energetic, and very ambitious. There was never a dull moment or a minute of down time—until I met him. For the first time in my life, I felt grounded. *He* grounded me, showed me how to relax, smell the roses, and sit long enough to find some quiet. I couldn't imagine my life without him in it.

I was no longer a single mom! I now had someone whom I trusted, loved, and respected by my side. I wanted to share all of my life with him, for the rest of my life. I hadn't been that happy in a really long time. He was smart and handsome, a great stepfather to my son, and he loved me with all of his heart ... it was truly magic!

It was a few months into our relationship when I knew I wanted this man in my life and that I just had to tell him about my condition. I described exactly what an SVT was, how the attacks affected me, and what his role needed to be if we were going to continue to grow our relationship. He of course was concerned, but not overly worried about them, until we experienced our first SVT attack together. It was about a year after we met. The longest I had ever gone previously without an SVT was three months! So, secretly, I was hoping that through meeting him and feeling true love and compassion, maybe I would be spared having any more attacks. I was wrong.

It was just after New Years. I was under a lot of stress, working long hours as I was in the beginning stages of opening my own real estate brokerage. My son, now in junior high school, helped out a little more around the home. But I was still juggling the pressures of owning a business, selling real estate, maintaining a house, and coping with the difficulties of blending my new relationship with my son. It was mid-evening and I knew that something was wrong.

My future husband and I were watching television after dinner when my head began to tingle as if I was going to faint. I lost my breath, and as I gasped for air, my husband looked at me as if I was choking. "What's wrong?!"

"Sweetie ... I'm having an SVT ... we have to go to the hospital ... I'm sorry," I said as calmly as I could. He panicked. It was like I'd said to him, "I'm having a baby and it's coming now!" He jumped up, quickly tried to help me off the couch, and began rushing me to the door. When I'm having an SVT, the blood doesn't pump very well, lowering my oxygen levels and making it hard for me to catch my breath. So his excitability in rushing, dragging, and pulling me was just making the situation worse. His main goal was to get me to the hospital, *now*!

I was calm but very disheartened. I thought to myself, discouragingly, "Here we go again." I told my future husband to call my son down from his room so I could say goodbye to him. By this time my son was around fourteen years old, and although he knew the risks, we were both confident that I would be home in a couple of hours.

As my future husband drove to the hospital, he was driving very slowly, trying gingerly not to hit any bumps. I calmly reminded him that *time was of the essence* and he needed to get me to a hospital as soon as safely possible. "Why the hell aren't we taking an ambulance?" he demanded.

"By the time an ambulance gets here, I can be at a hospital with an IV in my arm. It's just quicker this way ... and ... I don't have ambulance coverage and I'm too cheap to pay for it!" I joked. I was hoping that would lighten the mood a bit, but it only made it a topic for a discussion later on.

When we got to the hospital, he never left my side. As always, I was put in a small trauma room where the healthcare staff rushed around preparing to convert me. Everything was happening so quickly. One nurse was getting information from him, one nurse was putting an IV in my arm, one was putting on the blood pressure cuff, and one was taking my shirt off and sticking the small sensor sticky pads onto me to get an ECG reading. The on-call doctor was already at my bedside introducing himself and gathering my medical history. My future husband sat in awe, confused and overwhelmed by this whole situation. The look of worry and concern on his face prompted me to share with him a little more of how I was feeling. I tried to reassure him that everything would be all right ... I always am ... and I always convert without any problems.

While I am experiencing an SVT my mouth is very dry. My left arm tingles and aches and the fluttering feeling in my neck can be horribly uncomfortable. Occasionally, I can get a nasty headache and a sharp pain will start in my left armpit. I prefer to be in a semi-sitting position, as lying flat makes breathing a lot harder. For the most part, though, I am talkative, responsive, happy, and joking around, making a lame attempt to lighten up a serious situation. When the trauma room atmosphere is so serious and frantic, it makes converting tougher. Although I understand, appreciate, and respect the grave situation, sometimes caregivers only focus on the mechanics and not on the person. So by joking and fooling around I remind them that I am a person first, a patient second.

As my future husband watched the IV go in, some blood spilled out down my arm and onto the bed. The size of this IV needle is 18-gauge, which is very painful when it pierces my skin. It was once explained to me that an 18-gauge is almost as big as the lead within a pencil!

Once the needle was secured in my vein and taped to my arm, the doctor began putting the medicine into my IV to stop my heart momentarily. Before they administer the drug, they always remind me that cardioversion would be so much easier and much more beneficial for me ... and, of course, they promise I won't feel it! I always flatly and aggressively refuse. So, medicine it is.

By this time in my life, after having had so many SVT attacks, I was now limited to using only one medication, which was called *Adenosine*. The purpose of this drug is to stop my heart momentarily with the hope that it will then start up normally again. The downside with this drug is its lifespan. I was told that Adenosine has only a four-to six-second lifespan once it hits the bloodstream. So in order for this drug to be effective and make it to the heart within a few seconds, they push some water or saline solution immediately behind it to help it along. This is what medical staff will call an *IV push*.

The problem with this system is that it is administered by humans who are capable of error; and, some humans err more than others. After three attempts, if they can't get it right, then the doctor will refuse to administer any more medicine and will prepare and execute cardioversion to stop the SVT.

The IV push is a very tricky procedure. One person stands with the medicine and shoots it into the IV really quickly, while another must wait for the precise moment they are finished to send a big bolus of water to get it to the heart. All this must happen within seconds or the medicine is not effective and I remain in SVT. I've had this procedure botched so many times. Sometimes, the doctor in his arrogance is angry that I won't permit a cardioversion, so he will oversee a resident *attempt* this procedure. Most times their haphazard attempts fail, and they blame it on my irritable condition and proceed anyway with cardioversion. Again, I remain at their mercy.

Luckily for us that night I converted perfectly with the medication and it was a flawless performance by the hospital staff. It is a pretty scary and intimidating procedure for Larry to watch. Amazingly enough, this incredible man *still* has never left my side. Four years later, when my son was eighteen years old, Larry and I were married. With my son now grown and away from home, I am so blessed that my husband loves me dearly and continues to support me every day. He is truly my anchor.

Now that I was getting older, my SVTs were getting worse and happening more frequently. I found myself taking longer and longer to recover. The medication that once worked so well no longer seemed to have much effect on me. Cardioversion became more frequent, and the voltage of the shock continued to be increased. Although Larry knows what to expect he has never gotten used to my condition. It worries him terribly every time I whisper, "Sweetie, I'm having an SVT, we have to go."

The threat of a potential SVT episode looms over our lives every day. The threat is always present. Each time I get converted after an attack, without fail, Larry lovingly cups my hands in his and, with tear-filled eyes says, "I love you, I can't imagine my life without you." Then the process begins all over again.

Every day we happily live our life together, enjoying every minute of every day. We have accepted the nuisance of my condition because I always know in advance if I am going to have another SVT. However, there was one attack that was going to prove itself different, and prove me wrong ... one that neither my husband nor I will ever forget.

* * *

CHAPTER FIVE

Death's Door

While I thought that I was learning how to live,
I have been learning how to die.

~Leonardo da Vinci

It was the beginning of a beautiful autumn; the leaves were red, orange, and yellow and gently falling. The mornings were crisp with dew on the ground; the afternoons still provided the warmth of the earth and the sun still shone brightly. It was a gorgeous Saturday afternoon when my husband and I accompanied my sister and her husband to pick apples at our mom's house.

Although there were a lot of apples to pick and numerous bags to fill, it was such a great time just being together with family. I was brimming with renewed energy, and all of our time together was packed with great conversation and lots of laughter. Once the tree was picked clean, we all hugged, said goodbye, and headed back to our own lives. It was close to dinnertime and the activities of the day had left my husband and I too tired to cook. Although the fridge had been recently stocked with fresh groceries, we grabbed a burger and an ice cream cone on the way home. Even though our fabulous day was coming to an end, we were looking forward to our evening together. We had planned to relax and watch a couple of great movies.

After we finished watching our last movie, we began getting ready for bed. It had been such a great day and an even better evening. We lay in bed chatting for a few moments, reminiscing about the day's events. We were happy, life was perfect, and the day had been perfect. I was tired but grateful to be finally stretching out in bed. We were both looking forward to a good night's rest. Unfortunately, that rest never came.

It was in the early morning hours of Sunday, September 19, 2010, at 12:40 a.m. when my husband and I kissed goodnight and turned off the lights to go to sleep. I was lying on my back, and had just dozed off, when suddenly I felt horribly suffocated. It felt as if someone had put their large hand over my nose and mouth, prohibiting my breathing. I gasped for air and found myself in an SVT—this time without any warning. From the moment this attack started, it was very different from all the others. I was immediately unusually fearful. I felt a sense of impending doom and a silent *knowing* that I wasn't going to make it. As I had done so many other times before, I once again whispered, "Sweetie, I'm having an SVT, we have to go."

My husband was exhausted, and this was *not* how he had envisioned the rest of the night—another attack?! Why? We had enjoyed such an incredible, stress-free day! My husband rushed me once again to the hospital, thinking it was just another episode. He was hoping for a quick conversion so we could get back home and go to bed. With previous episodes, when we were on our way to the hospital, I was talkative. However, this time I couldn't seem to speak. I felt withdrawn, not in control, and very fearful. At the same time I felt a sense of wondering bewilderment.

Once we got to the hospital, as with all the other times, I told them I was having an SVT. However, on this particular night the emergency room was very busy. In the past, they normally rushed me right in and began preparing to convert me, but this time they needed to find some space and a bed for me. I tried to warn the nurse to *"get something happening, this is not going to go well for me."*

I sensed impending doom and feared that I was about to die. When this attack first began, my husband had thought that this was just another episode. But, by the look of concern and fear on *my* face, he knew that something was different this time.

After several minutes they made some room behind the nursing station triage desk. I was left to sit there for several more minutes while they tried to find space in a trauma bay, but with no success. I was wheeled to a small holding area in the recovery and rest section. I still didn't have an IV in my arm and no one was taking me seriously.

"Don't worry, everything is going to be fine," I was told. I felt so helpless, I *knew* I was going to die, and I desperately felt I could not let that happen. I was so scared and terrified that I would never see my son again. I never got to say goodbye to him, I thought. What were our last words together? Did I kiss and hug him when I last saw him? Why didn't I tell him I love him? Oh my God! How could *this* be happening to *me*?!

I had to get someone—anyone—to listen to me. For a split second I worried about how my death would affect my son. How would he make it without me? Who would comfort him? How could I widow my brand new husband? With everything we have been through, he had never left my side once, and now I was leaving his? We'd just gotten married....how was any of this fair?

This gut-wrenching sadness prompted me to fight harder. I got angry, quick-tempered, and belligerent, which only made matters worse. I was no longer the joking, laughing, happy patient they were used to seeing.

Because I have had so many of these episodes, many of the nurses knew *of* me. Most of them had treated me previously and weren't the least bit concerned that I wouldn't convert again ... after all, it was just another SVT. However, I knew otherwise.

I kept telling them, *"This is going to go real bad, real fast, do something now!"* A very young student nurse finally got around to putting an IV in my arm but neglected to tape it down, so it flopped around painfully. Another young student tried to hook me up to an ECG machine. Without heeding my panic and alarm about dying, they systematically continued with shaky confidence and reassurance that, as always, I would convert.

My husband had now clued in to the fact that this was not just another SVT and that something was very wrong. I felt horrible that I had no words of comfort or reassurance for my worried husband; I was too busy fighting for my life. As another new student tried to put the pads on me to hook me up to the ECG machine, she couldn't seem to put them in the right spot to get a reading. I was a frantic at this point, telling her that I was going to die and pleading for her to hurry up. Again, in hindsight, this only made matters worse. My helplessness was mounting; I couldn't seem to effectively impress my sense of impending doom on anyone.

My desperate pleas about dying were going unheard; they continued to take the situation in stride. After all, it was just another episode with a patient who presented often. The emergency room was packed with other traumas, and the hospital staff was overloaded and stretched far too thin. I didn't want to be that patient we all hear about *slipping through the cracks in the system*, because that meant I would be dead! They kept reassuring me that once a trauma room opened up I would be next, and not to worry, everything was going to be fine. But they were wrong....

A senior nurse rescued the inexperienced student from the ECG machine. Thankfully, she quickly and efficiently hooked me up to the machine. It began spitting out information that indicated I was in SVT. My heart was quivering at 223 beats per minute. I was clammy, sweating, and now gently vomiting. Based on what the ECG was telling the medical staff, it still looked like just another attack. My failed attempt to communicate that something else was drastically wrong still remained unheeded. My IV was still flopping in my arm, there was no foreseeable hope that I was going into a trauma room anytime soon, and no doctor probably even knew that I was there.

I began feeling lightheaded; the pain in my armpit and my neck was slowly starting to go away. It seemed I could think more clearly now. I held my husband's hand, telling him, *"I love you with all my heart; I am not going to make it."* I knew I didn't have long and I wanted to make the most of what I had. I wasn't angry anymore.

As I continued to vomit, I began losing control of my bowels and had an urgent need to urinate. Without warning, my blood pressure dropped to 56/27, and suddenly I heard them calling a *pre-code*. Once I realized the *pre-code* was me, I felt such relief. They finally understood my pleas for help and realized that I wasn't going to make it this time. Things started happening really quickly at this point for me. They rapidly wheeled my bed out of the recovery area and miraculously found a trauma room.

I told my husband, *"I think I'm going to die, but it's going to be okay."* I just wanted him to be prepared and not shocked. He said, "Don't talk like that, of course you're not going to die. Everything will be all right now."

Although in denial, we both secretly knew that this time was different. My husband and I both felt such relief that my deteriorating condition had finally been recognized. He felt hopeful that this horrible nightmare would soon come to an end. But for him the nightmare was really just beginning.

Somewhere between my anger, yelling, belligerence, and my current sense of relief, I no longer felt any fear about dying. Although I still knew that *I wasn't going to make it*, I no longer had any thoughts at all about how devastated my son or husband would be. I wasn't concerned that my untimely death would probably kill my aged mother, who relied on me for getting her groceries and cooking her meals. There were no thoughts of my family. I was no longer fighting for my life.

At this point, I was still in my conscious thinking mind. I still had my body and my brain working. I was not scared anymore. I was re-signed to the fact that I was going to die. I gave complete control to the nurses and doctors. However, I knew the outcome this time would be different.

As I sat up to vomit, I could feel the blood slowly begin to drain from my head. My whole body began to tingle, and I was slowly losing energy. The room started to go dim. As I looked around I could see my husband off to my side amongst numerous doctors and nurses.

The IV was still not in my vein correctly, so they inserted another one in my other arm and securely taped it down. There were so many doctors and nurses walking in and out of the room, making it impos-sible for me to keep track. A few came, and then left, while others seemed to linger by my bed just watching. The room was loud and fran-tically chaotic—organized confusion. Amongst a sea of lab coats my husband and I locked eyes.

I reached for his hand because the look of horror on his face was more than I could bear. We touched hands briefly. I whispered, *"I'm not going to make it."* He squeezed my hand, and with a quivering chin and large tears in his beautiful eyes, he said, *"I love you."* It was a silent know-ing between us that the situation had worsened. It was our fleeting mo-ment of goodbye.

Although I had fully surrendered to the doctors, and felt such relief that my plea had finally been heard, I knew without a doubt I was about to die. I was peaceful and totally okay with it. The last thing I remember was vomiting and begging the doctors to let me go to the bathroom. From that point on, I didn't know how many people were in the trauma room; I couldn't see my husband anymore. Then I heard someone telling me, "You're in good hands."

My last conscious brain thought was, "Yes, I am *going to Good Hands.*"

* * *

CHAPTER SIX

In Dad's Hands

Death is one of two things....
Either it is annihilation and the dead have no
consciousness of anything; or, as we are told, it is really a change:
a migration of the soul from one place to another.

~Socrates

The next thing I knew, I was standing by an orange cap in the trauma room. I was with my dad. He died in 2008. I didn't have the knowledge or a conscious thought that I was dead or that my father was dead. There was nothing conscious about this whole *way of being*. It is not like using your brain to process any thought. There are no words, labels, or names. It just is.

I did not see my dad's face. It was more like *knowing* that he was beside me. There is no seeing or even comprehension that you ever *could* see with your body's eyes, only the *known ability* to *sense* everything. There is no such thing as comprehension; and there is *no consciousness* that you ever possessed comprehension.

The best way to describe *sensing* is...*just knowing. Knowing* is done without intellectual logic or reasoning. I didn't have the *physical* identity of Lorri but I was still the *vibrational energy* of who I am.

We stood ... *stood* is the wrong word. It makes you think we had legs and feet, or that we were solid matter. We weren't. We didn't float or hover. We were just there. My dad and I were beside some orange cap. This cap felt like it was up high, and I *sensed* that there was a lot of energy (people) in the trauma room.

The people in the trauma room were not recognizable to me by their faces or their clothing. I sensed only their *vibrational energies*. I can best describe sensing the people in the room as like looking through the viewfinder of an infrared camera but without the colours within their shapes. I could see their bodies' shadowy outlines but couldn't tell if they were male or female, had light or dark skin, or what colour their hair was. All of these traits were indistinguishable.

From my vantage point, I could sense many individual *vibrational energy* outlines working on my body. I couldn't see myself but I knew that my body was there. My body, however, did not have an outline or energy like the others.

I could feel the intense *vibrational energy* from all of these people. Their energies felt loud; almost like striking a tuning fork really hard and drawing it close to your ear. The closer it gets, the louder it gets. Each person seemed to have a different pitch. Some were louder and more screechy, while others were soft and more pleasant. Among the loud energies there was one exception. It was a distinct, soft energy that was off to my left. I can best describe this energy as compassionate, empathetic, and kind, with a warm, distinct quietness.

The best way I can describe the intensity of *vibrational energy* is to compare it to the heat of a bonfire. The closer you go to the fire, the hotter it feels. Sensing the caregivers' collective *vibrational energy* was incredibly intense; it was definitely not a pleasant feeling. It was overwhelming, loud, and uncomfortable. My dad and I then left the trauma room.

To understand what I mean by "we *left* the trauma room," try to imagine not actually travelling from one spot to another. As quickly as

I found myself beside my dad in the trauma room, I was now just as quickly in another location. I don't know how I got there, or even where *there* was. It was like waking up and just *being*. It was a place of complete darkness, but I did not find it scary or fearful. Actually, I felt incredibly secure and very comfortable, almost like sitting downstairs in my own home.

This darkness was the most unimaginable *darkest blackness* that engulfed me with an all-encompassing familiarity, welcoming peacefulness, and complete stillness. Within this perfect indescribable quietness, I was in a state of fluid communication with my dad. It was a heightened state of *knowing or sensing*. Communicating with my dad was effortless. I had no mouth, lips, tongue, or voice box with which to communicate. I didn't know that a mouth, tongue, or voice box had ever existed! It was a supreme transfer of knowledge. There were no words, sentences, or voice inflections—just fluid, effortless communication. It was wonderful ... peaceful ... it was perfect. I couldn't actually smell my dad's cigarette smoke and his unique body odour, but I could *sense* at one point that it existed. Sensing his smell seemed perfectly comforting.

The feeling in this warm, *darkest blackness* was one of love, gentleness, happiness, blissfulness, softness, and tenderness. The words that I use to describe this space are so lame and hollow compared to what it was really like. It was right, it was perfect, and it was the way it should be. Please trust me when I tell you that being here felt perfectly natural and comfortingly familiar ... it was like coming home.

My dad had a message for me, but it was not communicated as our human minds can perceive it. There is no speaking. Communication happens without words, thoughts, or labels. Because his message was not communicated with words, it is difficult to describe because I must convert it into words so you can understand it. As I share his message with you, please understand that it sounds choppy, but the fluid transfer of information is quick communication and filled with unimaginable love. Within the conversion, I hope to capture his message without losing too much in the translation. This was his message:

> *His spiritual energy conveyed loving, nurturing, and reassuring contentment, both within him and me, then urged that I must go back—I refused. He transmitted encouragement, pride, loving, sweetness, long time left, work to be done, and then urged I must go back—again, I refused. Fluidly communicated happy of me, radiant, overwhelming in a great way, joy, tenderness, and glorious contentment, then demanded I cannot stay here any longer. I must go back ... NOW!*

When you are in this *energy* and on this level, you just know, understand, and accept that there is nothing physical about it. No touching, stroking, pinching, scratching—without any doubt, absolutely nothing physical about it. So when I sensed he was sending me back, I refused to go again. I wanted so badly to stay. I *needed* to stay. I needed the peace, the total fulfilling happiness, the unbelievable contentment, and the unconditional loving *perfectness* of it all.

I didn't have any conscious thought of a hospital. I had no conscious thought that I had a husband who was probably sick with worry and fear. I had no thoughts of my son, who would be totally devastated by the loss of his mom. I had no thoughts of my mom, brothers, or sisters ... anyone. I just really, really needed to stay in this *essence*. There was no conscious thought that I'd ever had human existence. There was certainly no conscious thought about sadness, worry, grief, anxiety, fear, or helplessness.

Being in this *spiritual essence* was not physical nor a dream; it was different. It was in the moment and filled with life. Even though I understood clearly that I couldn't stay, there was a sense of questioning wonderment as to whether my dad could really touch me to send me back. As my dad came close to me, I felt a very hard bump. I went through a really white tunnel. It was spiralling very, very quickly, and the white was blinding. It was a white so bright that your human eyes couldn't possibly stand to see it.

Time, as we know it here, doesn't exist there. There are no minutes or hours. Nothing has measurement, mass, weight, or volume. There are no deadlines and there is absolutely no rushing around. It is just forever! It is so peacefully perfect!

I had no conscious thought that the bump I felt was an indication I had been sent back. It was at this point that I opened my eyes; an image of my dad's face was on top of my husband's face. My dad wore glasses, but as I focused on him, he no longer had them on. I had always known my dad to have big, black, tired bags under his eyes, and now those tired black bags were gone. It was like the autofocus function on a camera. The lens would zoom in and out of focus, first on my husband's face, then on my dad's face. Once my dad's face faded, my husband's became clear. Although I was no longer in the peaceful *darkest blackness* of stillness, I thought I was still with my dad. Now, somehow, my husband was also here with us.

I had no idea I had a body again. I was trying to communicate with my husband as I had communicated with Dad. Although I was communicating effortlessly with my husband, he wasn't hearing me. I tried to share with my husband that I was so happy that he was here with us. In my mind I asked my husband, "Where is Dad?" but he didn't respond. I asked him, "Where are we?" Again, he didn't respond. I realized my husband couldn't hear me.

Why couldn't my husband communicate with me as my dad had? At this point I realized that I had a mouth, lips, and voice box and needed to use them so I could speak and communicate. Realizing that I'd have to physically speak, I said to my husband, "See Dad?" and "Where did Dad go?"

Larry didn't say anything, so I said, "I saw Dad." My husband, with tear-filled eyes, then quietly asked, "How is he?" I got terribly upset by this and very frightened because if my husband *was* with me, he should know how Dad is. If my husband *wasn't* with us, where the hell am I? Where is Dad? What the hell is happening?

It struck me that I didn't know where I was. Which level am I on? Where did I go? How long was I there? Why is my husband so upset? Why am I back here? Something is wrong! I wanted so badly to go back to where I was. I was so disappointed to physically see my body and physically feel the pain in my body. But something was very different; my hearing seemed amplified and my vision was crystal clear.

Everything in the trauma room was so loud and bright. Everything around me seemed different than I remembered, but my body looked exactly the same. I could still sense the *vibrational energy* of the people around me, but the intensity was different and a lot louder. There was no more peace or recognizable stillness. There was no indescribable love or gentleness. It was as if everyone were talking very loudly but not moving their lips.

Everything seemed to be so noisy, almost deafening. My eyes could see everything more vividly. It was too bright and very uncomfortable. My sense of smell was very acute, which made me feel nauseated. I wanted nothing more than to go back. "Where am I?" I asked my husband.

"You're in the hospital," he said.

"What happened?" I asked.

My husband said, "You had an SVT."

In my brain, I'm thinking that none of this is making any sense. "Where is Dad?" I asked again. I still didn't realize that my dad was dead. My husband never responded, and I knew then with all certainty that something was terribly wrong. When I asked the question "Where am I?" I wanted to know if I was here or back there.

When I questioned *what happened*, I meant, what happened to the *darkest blackness* of perfect, quiet, stillness, and what happened to Dad? The look on my husband's face said it all. He looked as if he had been crying. I could see such relief and joy in his face as he looked at me.

Still not knowing where I was, I asked again, "Where am I?"

"You're in the hospital."

"What happened?"

"You had an SVT." Larry reminded.

"Where is Dad?" I asked yet again.

Then my husband's sad but joyous face took on the most worried expression I had seen. He told me that I had asked the same questions for almost ten minutes. He'd started to think that I was going to be like "Ten Second Tom" from the movie *50 First Dates*!

I slowly started to realize that I was no longer on that other level. I was now back here. Why? All I could think of was going back to be with Dad again in that wonderful *darkest blackness*, but I didn't know where *back* was. I just knew that I wanted to be *there* and not *here*.

I began to sob as the realization hit me that my dad was dead, and that he had been so for quite some time. Slowly I started to remember the details of coming to the hospital for an SVT, but I didn't have *all* the details. After what the nurses and my husband told me, I was shocked to realize that *they* had all the dirty details.

* * *

CHAPTER SEVEN

Why Am I Here?

What is, is.
What isn't, isn't.
When you become so obsessed with what isn't
you miss what is.

~Unknown Author

As I lay on that metal hospital bed, I could feel the pain in my body. I knew that everything was different. My husband snuggled up close to my right side; with his one hand he tenderly stroked my arm, and with his other he ran his fingers through my hair. He was careful not to touch the large IV that was still painfully embedded in my arm.

Everything was so loud, and very bright. I could still feel the *vibrational energies* of people in the room. Now, however, I could visually recognize them. They were no longer just outlines. The orange cap turned out to be the lid of a disposable container on a shelf in the trauma room, but it wasn't as high up as I'd thought. It was definitely the cap, but the view I'd seen was not indicative of where it was hanging on the wall. Why was that?

Where I had stood with my dad by the orange cap, I saw a nurse at a computer terminal. I recognized the same soft energy that I'd seen with Dad. Only this time, she had distinctive features. I asked my husband as I was pointing toward the nurse in the corner, "Has she always been here?" Smiling, my husband said, "Yes, she gave me a chair while we were losing you. She told me to sit down before I fell down!"

This was the first realization I had that something had happened to me. Unlike me, my husband and the medical team had watched the whole thing from a different viewpoint. According to my husband, my blood pressure dipped dangerously low, they sedated me, the doctors ran into complications as they electronically defibrillated me, and I quit breathing. They frantically tried to revive me.

They were yelling my name, rubbing my sternum and forcing oxygen into my lungs, hoping to stimulate breathing. My poor husband watched in horror as I was seconds away from having a breathing tube inserted. Over a minute later, I began to breathe slowly on my own. The entire episode might have only lasted five to seven minutes, but it was the longest few minutes of my husband's life!

After I stabilized, I began to tell the medical team where *I* had gone and what *I* had seen. It was as if we were all comparing notes about a horrible accident, all from different vantage points. As I was trying to mentally understand what had happened to me and grasp why I felt so different, the nurses suspected what had happened but wanted more information. So the more they asked, the more I told them, and the crazier it sounded. The crazier it sounded, the more they wanted, but the more fearful I got.

I still did not realize that the peaceful, perfect stillness of *darkest blackness* was death. I didn't have a name for what had happened to me, and I didn't really care to figure it out or put a label on it. I just wished I could go back to the perfect stillness that I had come from. I still did not comprehend that I had just survived a *near-death experience*, or what that meant.

I was in shock, and at the same time I felt fearful and confused that my body could look the same while everything else was so different. Then, finally, one of the nurses explained in detail the symptoms of a near-death experience; she'd been reading a book on it. She wrote down the name of the book with its author and suggested that I read it but she said nothing about the after-effects. But I scoffed at the idea, because I'd just realized there was no such thing as death, so why should I read it!?

At that moment, I knew I was different physically, mentally, emotionally, and spiritually. When I left the hospital, I knew that I was no longer the same person I had been. I knew that I'd survived a life-altering experience called a *near-death experience*. Although my husband was overjoyed that I was alive, I wasn't grateful at all. Why me?

Without my realizing it, this was the beginning of denial, fear, and curiosity. I was filled with overwhelming resentment and anger that I had been sent back. I thought I was being punished. "Why would I be allowed to feel such peace and joy only to be sent back here?" This *here* is not a nice place to be. I was tormented by having touched paradise only to have it ripped away from me. It felt like such a terrible tease, a cruel joke that was not funny at all, and I was angry with the entire world!

After I left the hospital, and in the days following my near-death experience, I was still recovering at home. My feelings of anger and resentment were compounded by my guilt at the ungratefulness I felt for still being alive. I became very self-absorbed and thought obsessively about that night, and I developed indescribable insecurities. The horrible fear of being called crazy locked me into denial and secrecy; I chose never to share any aspect of this experience. I passionately, secretly hoped that as time passed and my physical body healed, these changes *would* eventually go away. My hopes soon vanished that I would return to *normal* ... little did I know that this was only the beginning of *not* being normal.

My body felt as if it had been battered and abused. I felt as if I had been in a horrible accident that I shouldn't have survived. Where the doctor did the sternum rub on my chest, it was very sore and felt painful to the touch. I had burn marks from the defibrillator pads. My ribs felt as if they were broken, and it was difficult to breathe deeply. As a result of air having been forcibly pushed into my lungs to stimulate my breathing, my chest hurt every time I took a breath. When the doctors pushed a breathing mask hard on my face to ensure they had a good seal, it felt as if they had broken my nose. They pressed on my jaw so aggressively that they pushed a vertebra out of place in my neck.

My teeth were sore, my ribs were sore; my whole body ached as if I had been dropped from a plane. I was still physically exhausted, but my mind had never been more alive. I was mentally firing on all cylinders. As my body was healing, I noticed many changes in my demeanour, my personality, my character, my mind, and my thoughts. Some of the changes I really enjoyed and sort of hoped would stay, but the rest of the changes left me feeling so frightened that I would have goose bumps and be sweating at the same time!

It had been about a week since I'd come home from the hospital. My husband and I had the best cut of AAA steaks sitting in the fridge, so we decided that we would enjoy a wonderful barbeque dinner. Getting up and around, finally doing something was refreshing; it felt great getting back into a routine. I began baking the potatoes, cleaning and cutting up some fresh mushrooms and onions so I could sauté them together. Simultaneously, I was also preparing some fresh vegetables to have with our dinner; it was going to be a lovely meal.

I got the package of steak out of the fridge so I could season the meat for my husband to cook. As I picked up the package and proceeded to open it, something weird happened.

At the smell of blood I became so nauseated I thought I was going to vomit. My mouth filled with salty water and my stomach started to heave. Although the meat looked perfect and was within the "best before" date, I thought maybe it had spoiled. I couldn't stomach opening the package, so I called my husband and asked him to prepare the steaks. I finished preparing the rest of the meal without any problems.

Once Larry opened the steak package and began seasoning them,

I again smelled blood and got very nauseous. My husband could not smell a thing and eagerly anticipated a wonderful dinner. Once the dinner was cooked and ready to eat, all I could smell was this nauseous, rank odour of blood that curdled my stomach.

With horrible fear of being called *crazy*, I timidly shared my disgust for the steak with my husband, who said, "Well, maybe it's a good thing. Right now your body is healing, and meat may be too hard for you to digest. Your body must be telling you that red meat is not what it is craving." He proceeded to comfort me: "I really wouldn't worry about it; you'll eat a steak whenever you're ready." What he probably was thinking was, "Mmmmm ... I get her leftovers!"

This got me thinking ... more than anything, *I* wanted to enjoy that beautiful barbequed steak, but my *body* didn't? I understood what my husband had meant, but my brain controls my body, not the other way around. So, if it is my brain that doesn't want steak anymore, why? It had to be something logical, since we were talking about the brain. Could it be the medication they gave me when I was at the hospital? Or when they shocked me, did it knock something loose? Or maybe I was really going crazy! "Yeah, you're probably right," I agreed. "It will probably go away, when my body is healed," and I didn't give it any more thought after that. The only thing my body craved and couldn't get enough of was fruit! Any type of fruit; but woman can't live on fruit alone ... I sure tried though!

After the first couple of weeks since my experience, I *sensed* everything as if the volume was cranked up. The only person I had any physical contact with was my husband. If something would make him mad ... or happy ... or sad, I could sense it like a cold breeze slapping me hard then screaming in my face. Everything seemed so loud to me, like what you might experience if you had a horrible head cold. The music I once enjoyed now sounded like nails on a chalkboard. I absolutely couldn't be around any noise. This horrible sensitivity to sound and to light forced me to retreat to any quiet, dark place I could find in the house. I loved my husband with all of my heart, but for some reason, I couldn't stand to be near his *vibrational energy*; even it was too loud!

I missed him so much, his touch, his smell, and the way we used to share and laugh together. I was grieving. I was grieving the loss of being normal, eating red meat, but more importantly, I was grieving the loss of the loving, bonding, connection my husband and I had once shared. Since coming home from the hospital, I hadn't left the house or really talked with anyone. I functioned best when I was alone and the house was perfectly quiet and dark. I alienated myself from everyone, including the love of my life. I created my own little world in which I was very much alone but perfectly peaceful.

In those quiet moments I prayed as much as I cried. I had nothing else *to* do. Why me, God? What did I do to deserve this? Why are you punishing me? I wondered how I would ever function in society again. The minutes and the hours of my days all blended into one; time didn't exist for me anymore. Alone by my choosing, I cried and prayed to God, Why am I here? But *He* never answered me.

* * *

CHAPTER EIGHT

I'm Crazy!

Life has meaning only in the struggle.
Triumph or defeat is in the hands of the gods.
So let us celebrate the struggle!

~Sri Swami Sivananda

After about three weeks, my physical body was healed, but the changes I feared hadn't gone anywhere. My excessive consumption of fruit remained. I no longer had any burn marks, my ribs and my jaw were no longer sore, and it was easier to take in deep breaths. The only lingering evidence of having this experience was that the back of my neck was still pretty tender and that I was physically exhausted all of the time.

My husband and I were both real estate agents running our business out of our home. I was not able to work yet, so my husband was doing everything. Needless to say, the pressure of running a real estate career for two, paying bills, keeping a home, getting groceries, cooking dinner, and worrying about a sick wife was starting to seriously take its toll on him. I did not spend a lot of time with him and our relationship was deteriorating rapidly. Most times, as he would walk silently into my room, I already felt as if he was screaming. So I would leave the room, hoping he wouldn't follow.

One night, coming to bed, he said to me, "I know we are in the same house together and we are home all day long ... but I miss you. I don't know who you are anymore ... I love you and I want my wife back." I started to cry. I knew exactly what he was talking about. I missed him so dearly. I missed *myself* so dearly. Then it dawned on me ... he is not loud anymore ... it's quiet ... why?

I hugged him so hard and was sobbing in his arms. I felt so lost and had no idea why. I wanted nothing more than to explain to him how I was feeling, but there just didn't seem to be the right words. How do you explain to your soul mate that he is too *loud* when you're in a room filled with silence? How do you tell the love of your life that you now can't stand his *energy* and you don't know what the hell that means?

I felt so lost, inadequate, and helpless. I knew we were in love with each other and I just had to try to explain it, no matter how crazy it sounded. As I lay in his arms on the bed, I began describing this loudness: "It's like when the television is too loud and you are not sitting by the remote control to turn it down. The noise quickly becomes very annoying, almost agitating. Or it's like having the worst migraine headache but being forced to work on a construction site on a bright summer day. That is how I feel with *everything*! I feel so frustrated and over-stimulated because I don't know how to turn it down, and all I want to do is cry like a baby."

While he was sitting with me, I realized that he didn't seem loud anymore. I told him that it felt like the same *vibrational energy* I felt when standing with my dad in the hospital's emergency room that night. The only difference now was that I could see my husband's body. How could that be?

We decided that night that no matter what I was feeling, no matter how crazy it sounded, we needed to get to the bottom of this. He said, "When I feel *loud* to you, just tell me and I will try to figure it out.

No matter what *weird* feeling you're having, tell me so I can try to understand it." From that moment on, my quest began. I felt confident I was going to get some answers, or at least a reasonable explanation.

Watching in horror as I died that night, my husband got to see and feel firsthand how really fragile life is. He now appreciated that our lives were not to be taken for granted. He was so thankful that we were still here together. There were so many things we still needed to do, so many things to see and beautiful places to discover. He was filled with a sense of a new beginning, a fresh start. I was scrambling.

JOURNAL ENTRY: October 14, 2010 10:30 a.m.

"How the hell am I going to get through this? I used to have a husband and a life with a normal job, now I can't seem to function. Why me? How is this even fair? What did I do to deserve this? What if I am never able to leave the house again? How is this fair to my husband? ....

Today is a bit better of a day, we had a good talk last night and surprisingly he seems softer. Why? Maybe all of this is in my head. Maybe I am going crazy. I miss him so much, I miss me so much. What the hell happened to me? Where did I go? How much longer will he take this bullshit before he leaves, although I can't say I would blame him ... I would probably leave me too....

If I tell him everything that I am feeling, he will think I am crazy and he will leave. If I don't tell him everything, I can't stand to be around him ... so I will leave. Either way it looks like our bright and happy future planning to live life blissfully in retirement sounds more like divorce than bliss right now ... how cruel, how sad. This is what I have become."

I put so much pressure on myself to find my *old normal* and to try to pick up where I had left off. But when your *old normal* dies, a *new normal* is automatically born. It doesn't mean that you will automatically *recognize* that a *new normal* exists, but it will become very clear that you will not be able to function in *old normal,* no matter how hard you try. That was one of the hardest lessons I've had to learn.

Until I was prepared to let go of the *old normal,* I would never be able to see anything *new*. It is in *letting go* that we *find*. It is our fear and denial that we refuse to let go. However, my new normal *caused* me fear, confusion, pain, and chaos, which put me in denial. Who would readily accept that?

My husband and I began spending more time together and were talking a lot about what had happened. I was comfortable sharing some of the crazy things I was feeling and what was happening around me. For example, any time we would watch television, the channel display would come up on the screen like someone was trying to change it. It was a little unnerving at first, but we soon got used to it, thinking that the remote control must have an electrical short in it. Another odd thing was that our light bulbs kept burning out. Strangely enough, in one month three inside oven lights had burned out, and I wasn't even cooking! My cordless phones died very easily, clocks would just stop working, or my husband's cell phone would randomly light up as if someone were calling.

It had been almost a month since I had left the house. One day my husband tried to persuade me that it was time to try to get out. "It's not healthy to stay cooped up like this. I have to go grocery shopping. Come with me." It didn't sound as if I had much choice. So my first outing was tagging along to get some groceries. As we left the house, it felt like the world was so much bigger and I was so much smaller in comparison. Everything was so alive, humming with energy, it was im-possible to take it all in.

As we entered the store, my husband grabbed a cart and I was holding onto his arm, more for protection than stability. The *vibrational energy* of all the people in the store was bellowing loud. I felt like a small, shy child in a massive group of people, hiding behind my mother's skirt. I held tightly to my husband's arm, walking slightly behind him, using him as a shield.

"What's wrong?" he asked.

"I don't know … I think I'm just tired," I said. Even though lying probably wasn't the best policy, I needed more time to figure this *loudness* out.

"We don't need much, we'll go soon," he said, doing his best to comfort me.

At that moment, my husband had a very peaceful energy about him in comparison to what I was experiencing from the other shoppers. I needed my "shield" to stay as peaceful as he could until I could get out of there. As we were walking around and picking up a few items, I was slowly remembering the night in the hospital, when I could feel the medical team's *vibrational energy*. Now, all the shoppers' energies were very similar, in that I could feel them in the same way. But the intensity was louder and I couldn't escape it. I began to figure out that each person has their own intensity of energy, like that of a tuning fork, only louder. This energy was not the type of energy I used to feel before my near-death experience. It was more like the energy I felt when I was dead. How could this be?

In the previous month, he'd been buying me several fruit platters each week. I was so pleased that, for the first time since my experience, I got to pick out my own fruit platter. As I was leaning over a refrigerated shelf, another shopper joined me and was looking at the same fruit platters. As she came near me and leaned over the refrigerated shelf, I got a very quick snippet of a picture of her screaming at small children who were so little and crying near her feet. I gasped as I looked at her. Apparently, I was staring at her but all I could see was this image in my head. "What the hell is wrong?" my husband said, as if I was crazy.

"Sorry...," my husband said apologetically to the woman as he picked up a fruit platter and ushered me away. As I was walking away I noticed a small child inside her cart with miscellaneous grocery items. I was stammering to explain, "She seemed nice on the outside ... but she feels mean ... like yelling at kids ... she was mean...." He didn't say a word, he didn't have to. I knew instantly my husband was embarrassed.

After forty minutes of shopping we paid for our groceries and were leaving the store. I realized that I was slowly beginning to figure it out. The *energy* that I feel on the outside of a person isn't the same *vibrational energy* that I feel from inside them. The incongruity of these two conflicting feelings leaves me bewildered and sometimes fearful. It was the fear of feeling these opposing energies that had kept me from leaving the security of my home.

In the situation with that woman, I didn't know if that child in the cart belonged to her or if she even screams at all. All I know is that what I saw wasn't very nice. I don't believe that she was a mean or bad person. I thought that, just as my husband's energy could change, so can hers. At that moment in time, her energy seemed hostile and aggressive, which caught me off guard. Unable to prove anything, I reasoned that it was part my imagination, part fatigue, and part real.

JOURNAL ENTRY: October 16, 2010 8:45 p.m.

Holy sh*t, what a day! My first outing and I am such an embarrassment. He used to be proud of me; now I can feel his disgust and shame in me. He doesn't understand and it's not my fault. How is it my damn responsibility to make him? He thinks he has it bad? Try living in my f*cking body. Try hearing the voices I hear. Try knowing that sh*t is going to happen before it happens. And he feels like he has it so bad. What about me? ....

In my fifteen-year real estate career I have probably met hundreds of people. I can easily say that upon meeting each one of those people, I never felt anything like what I can feel today. I can feel the outside misery and pain that many are going through, but I can also go to the core and feel each one's beauty, peace, and love.

I knew after that grocery shopping trip that something very profound, real, and different had happened to me. My near-death experience had altered me, leaving my life and my husband's life in horrible discord. Although my husband wanted to help me figure out what was happening, at times it was too much for him.

I wasn't sure where these changes were coming from or if I was *ever* going to change back. All I really knew was that I was starting to spiral downward. I cared very little about anything anymore. I didn't have the will power to figure it out, and each day a little piece of me was being eaten alive; I knew that, soon, there would be nothing left. I didn't care, either. I was either crazy, gifted, exhausted, or had one hell of an imagination. The only thing I cried for was peace, which could only be found in death....

CHAPTER NINE

I Don't Want to Be Here Any More!

"Let not your heart be troubled: ye believe in God, believe also in me.
In my Father's house are many mansions: if it were not so,
I would have told you. I go to prepare a place for you."

~Gospel of John 14:1–2, 27

Eight months after my near-death experience, my life was still in utter chaos, and I felt like I no longer *fit*. In deep despair and having suicidal thoughts, I regularly voiced to my husband my distaste with life and my desire to leave it. It was not surprising that my husband and I sadly began growing apart. I was crying all the time, wanting the *old Lorri back*, wanting my old life back. Although I looked exactly the same, my husband and I knew instinctively that something was very different about me. I often thought that if it were my destiny to have a near-death experience, then I wished I could have been physically mangled in an accident. At least then the changes I felt on the inside would match the changes on the outside. That would justify having the sensitivities that frightened me and would excuse my odd behaviour.

Because of my unexplained freaky sensitivities, I no longer left the house, which meant that I was no longer working. We had a very large home and I was not able to maintain it, so we decided to sell it before summer. I happily gave almost all of our belongings and furniture away and moved into what we thought would be a quiet condo close to the hospital. As if matters couldn't get any worse, my cardiac condition became increasingly dangerous. *Any* fluctuation in my heart rate or blood pressure would easily trigger an SVT. Our trips to the hospital were now happening almost every three weeks! The medication that had once been effective no longer worked. Ironically, cardioversion became my best friend. Every time the medical staff would hook me up to zap the daylights out of me, I prayed for death. Yet, it seemed that the more I denied my fearful sensitivities, the louder and more pronounced they got.

Things "*unexplained*" riddled my behaviour to the point that I just didn't care anymore what people thought. In addition to my heightened sense of hearing, one of the weird sensitivities was my sickeningly acute sense of smell. I could smell things that didn't seem to be there. I would ask my husband, "I smell my dad's cigarette, do you smell that?"

My husband, being very logical, would say, "No, how do you know it's your dad's cigarette and not the neighbour's or from someone outside?" I was frustrated because I *sensed* I smelled it. It's a different type of *knowing*. Because he couldn't relate to what I could *sense*, he would try to give it a logical explanation in the hope that this might somehow help me. But for me, this seemed to reinforce the notion that something was wrong with me. More often than not, sensing a smell meant something. Usually I could figure it out immediately, but sometimes it wasn't until weeks after that I got the message.

Similar to my sense of smell, my snippets of mental pictures were like precognition, but also, as I like to call it, *pre–déjà vu*. They did not seem to be in my *conscious mind*. What I mean is that I couldn't will myself to create these snippets of pictures and they seemed outside of my control. It was a very large source of fear for me. At any second I could get a snippet of a picture which made no sense at all. It was random, vivid, and one that you would know but couldn't explain. It left me feeling lost, anxious, and insecure, as if I was going crazy. Was this in my mind or my imagination? Why would I imagine something like this? I needed to understand these pictures and I needed to learn how to live with them. The *pre–déjà vu* snippets of pictures didn't seem to be going away or subsiding. Then one day ... I figured it all out.

One day, before we sold our home, my husband and I were going grocery shopping, which was the only place he could get me to go. As I bent over to put my shoes on, a picture flashed of my husband driving my vehicle with me beside him. This didn't make any sense. Other than my first day out, I always drove my own vehicle. This picture frustrated me and I proceeded to ignore it.

We closed the door, locked the house, and went shopping. As I was getting out of my vehicle at the shopping center, I got another picture of my husband's hand in slow motion putting my car keys on a shelf in our garage by the garage door opener button. It made me stop for a second. Then I saw it again except faster this time. "Enough is enough," I thought. I made a decision to pay attention to any pictures that I would get. As soon as I would see the pictures they would go away almost as if I had never remembered them. They were so quick that I couldn't seem to translate what I saw into words to tell my husband.

While we were shopping, I knelt down to get a can of soup off the bottom shelf. While I reached for the soup I saw myself standing on the top step inside my garage, in front of the garage door which enters into our home. I could see my husband standing on the garage floor and I was yelling at him to "Calm down!" It just kept playing over and over.

"What's wrong ... what are you looking at?" my husband asked. I stood up and explained exactly what I saw. I didn't remember the two other pictures at that time. I was adamant about what I saw. As we were in the lineup, I got another picture. I saw my husband and me standing outside our bedroom window. It was slightly open and we were both looking up at it. He was fuming mad, which was rare for my husband. Then I saw this picture again but in slow motion.

"Hello, Earth to Lorri ... whatcha' thinkin' 'bout?" he asked. I explained it to him in great detail. "That doesn't make any sense, why would I be mad if our window was open? Could you make out if it was broken?" he laughed. I didn't think it was funny at all. I started to feel a little lightheaded and exhausted.

The blood drained from my face, leaving me concerned that I was going to faint. Grudgingly still angry with him for joking, I knew he had to drive us home. As we were driving home I began to feel a bit better but I still gave him the cold shoulder for his poor choice of a joke.

As my anger and frustration with him subsided, I turned to look at him to say something, and then, like a déjà vu, I remembered that I had "seen" this already. It felt strange yet comforting and confusing all at the same time. I just stared at him as if something else was missing. It was like only hearing half a sentence and anxiously anticipating the rest.

"What?" he asked.

"I did this already ... do you feel like you did this too?"

"No," he said, with a puzzled look on his face. As we drove up the driveway and pulled into the garage, I saw another picture. I watched my fingers push the keyless entry on the garage door to gain access to the house. Then I tossed my keys on the dryer as I walked through the back door. This was out of character for me, as I never opened the keyless entry when I was with my husband. After our last conversation, I refused to share this little picture with him. He would probably ridicule that too.

My husband began loading up his arms with the groceries that we had just bought. He walked up the steps to the garage door and pushed the keyless entry so we could get into the house. To both our dismay, the batteries had died and the keyless entry was useless. Since we'd taken my vehicle, my husband did not have his keys with him. His key chain was the only one that had a house key on it.

He quickly ran to the front door with my set of keys to open it. Realizing the deadbolt was locked from the inside and that I didn't have a house key on my key ring, he came back to the garage highly irritated. By this time I was standing on the top step of the garage, and in slow motion I watched my husband's hand put my car key ring on the top shelf in the garage by the garage door opener button.

"I did this! I saw this already!" I was so excited, but very confused. It was like a déjà vu except in advance. I was so overwhelmed in the moment that I wasn't the least bit concerned that we were locked out.

My husband was furious that I did not have a house key on my car key chain. He became angrier that I didn't seem to share his same frustration. He was ranting about how we had to call a locksmith and would probably have to wait two hours. My already super-sensitive hearing was tilting with all his ranting, to the point that I just screamed, "Calm down!... It's just a lock, for Pete's sakes!"

I quietly gasped, and by the apparent shocked look on my face, my husband said, "What? Do you know where a key is...?"

"No. Why?"

Now he was even angrier.

"Well, you looked like you remembered something or had a good idea."

There was nothing I could say or do to comfort him. He was frustrated and that was how he would stay until we could gain access to the house. If I told him that I'd already seen this he would probably pop his top!

On our way to the backyard to check the back door, we passed by our bedroom window, which was open slightly. We both stood there for a moment, as we looked up at it surmising whether we could get in through its tiny opening. Instantly, as I stood there, I remembered that I had remembered this.

"We did this already ... do you remember what I told you when we were standing in the lineup? You thought it was funny. You were mad and the window was open."

I knew what I'd seen earlier; now it made perfect sense. I was so pleased with myself that I was slowly putting the puzzle pieces together. Hoping my husband would share my jubilation that I wasn't crazy, he said, "Well, do you have any snippets of pictures of how we get back in?"

I had such hurt feelings for being mocked when I knew I was on the right track. But, I suppose, who could blame him?

"As a matter of fact I do," I told him. "I remember touching the keyless entry and tossing my keys on the dryer. So that would mean we must have gotten in."

We were still standing outside our bedroom window arguing. "Really ... did you see a clock in your picture? Maybe what you saw happened a month ago. Who is to say that it was today? Maybe it's just wishful thinking." Now I was angry! No one is going to tell me what I know. I know what I saw. I know what it meant. As I stormed off to try the keyless entry one more time, a little insecurity came over me. I began to doubt myself. Insecurity turned quickly to fear. I was not fearful of being wrong; I was fearful of being ridiculed.

When I reached the door, and as I put my hand near the keyless entry, I knew I was right. As I punched the buttons on the keyless entry, the deadbolt slowly, sluggishly unlatched. I picked up my keys from the top part of the shelf and tossed them on to the dryer.

From that moment on, I knew whatever I saw would come true. I never doubted myself again ... nor did my husband! My husband is now a full believer; how can he not be? Although he *has* asked me to pick out the winning lottery numbers, I lovingly remind him that *this* is not how it seems to work!

As the days turned into weeks, I continued to share with my husband the *paranormal* changes I was experiencing. These changes were very uncomfortable, confusing, unnerving, and often frightening. But the piece that had locked me into denial and suicidal thoughts was that I did not know where these changes were coming from. The aspect of the *unknown* solidly reinforced the feeling that I probably would *never* be *normal* again! So how do you fight the *unknown*? You find it and make sense of it; you make the *unknown* ...*known*!

I knew what I was feeling was real, but I did not know where it came from. Was it in my mind, my body, or my spirit? Was it a combination of all three? I didn't know if I needed a psychotherapist, a medical doctor, a psychic, or a priest! To my surprise, it was none of the above.

* * *

CHAPTER TEN

Time for Change

When we are no longer able to change a situation
we are challenged to change ourselves.

~*Viktor Frankl (Man's Search for Meaning)*

Before my near-death experience, like you, I could feel someone's mood by using one of my five senses. I considered myself a successful person, happily married to whom I believed to be my *only* soul mate. I cherished the bond with my son and I marvelled at the power of a mother's love. As a real estate agent and businesswoman, I loved my job and *most* of the people I dealt with. I never used to hear any voices or give much thought to déjà vu. When a great song came on the radio, I thought nothing of cranking up the volume and singing along. Possibly much like you, the thought of dying scared the hell out of me because I still had so much to do. Experiencing the gut-wrenching loss of a loved one would leave me grief-stricken and would momentarily pique my curiosity about death and an afterlife.

But after my near-death experience I was different. My life was different. The goals, dreams, and hopes that I once envisioned had vanished. I no longer cared about money or paying bills, relationships took on a greater meaning, and the hours and minutes within each day stood still—time had no meaning for me. But, ironically enough, I could *never* have imagined that this degree of emotional upheaval would have such devastating and crippling effects on me and my family's life. The pain of depression is unfathomable; and until you walk in those shoes, it will remain unfathomable to you.

There came a moment, a huge moment of realization, that these sensitivities were not getting any better and they didn't appear to be going away anytime soon. I knew that I *must* make a change. A conversation with my older sister sparked something within me to make the right decision. Since I knew these heightened sensitivities started after my near-death experience, I needed to know why they were here. Would they *ever* go away? From where did they originate: my mind or a Higher Power? This prompted me to do a great deal of research into the physical and mental after-effects of a near-death experience.

I found many qualified resources on the research and development of NDE knowledge. I have spent countless days and weeks exploring research from many different sources, such as books, websites, author interviews, and research articles. Being a near-death survivor, I automatically seem to know if the information I read is accurate. If it resonates with me then I consider it to be solid. If the information does not resonate with me then I do not promote or quote from that source. This is not to say that the information is not correct. It is merely to say that if it doesn't *feel* right, then why would I pass it on to you?

There are many wonderful resources and fabulous authors who have devoted their life's research to the phenomenon of NDE. I give special recognition to all these sources, such as Dr. P.M.H. Atwater, Dr. Raymond Moody, the Near-Death Experience Research Foundation (NDERF), and the International Association for Near-Death Studies (IANDS).

All of these sources helped me to understand my new chaos after my NDE. The information from IANDS really resonated with me, as I found it to be the most fascinating and stunningly accurate site. According to the IANDS website...

Around eighty percent of the people who experienced near-death states claimed that their lives were forever changed by what happened to them.... Experiencers were not returning with just a renewed zest for life and a more spiritual outlook. They were evidencing specific psychological and physiological differences on a scale never before faced by them.

This reassured me that I was not going crazy, and surprisingly, the changes I felt were both in my mind and in my body. I was so relieved that the changes I felt had been felt by others who have also survived a near-death experience. *This* was normal, it was _my new normal_. Interestingly enough, P.M.H. Atwater echoed the same evidence based on her research. Atwater (1996) stated:

... *not just the* psyche is affected by the near-death phenomenon. A person's body and the very way life is lived undergo changes too. Mundane chores can take on surrealistic dimensions.

Several researchers were also in agreement and stated the same facts. Based on the reports of their near-death survivor accounts, IANDS research reported the same sort of physical changes. Some of the distinctive physical after-effects of a near-death experience are described:

Sensitivity to light and sound can be a serious issue and may necessitate some lifestyle changes. Almost everyone, though, has similar difficulties with loud or discordant sounds. Many can no longer tolerate "hard" rock music.

Reading about this sensitivity to light and sounds made me feel reassured that it was a change that many others have felt. After countless weeks of reading all this material, I slowly began to get comfortable with my new self. I began to no longer feel so foreign, and I was settling down and not fighting these changes as much. Like Atwater,

IANDS goes on to explain about the television remote and the light bulbs burning out. The IANDS website describes it best:

Electrical sensitivity refers to a condition whereby the force field or energy around an individual affects nearby electrical equipment and technological devices. . .some experiencers have noticed: watches can stop, microphones "squeal," tape recorders quit, television channels change with no one at controls, light bulbs pop, telephone "drops off," computers suddenly lose memory, and so forth. Experiencers more at ease with their new traits report fewer of these incidents than those still in the process of making adjustments.

It was well over six months now and I still couldn't bear to smell red meat, let alone touch it! Why? Was this still my brain telling me I didn't like red meat any longer? My body violently didn't want to have any part of it. Interestingly, all the research that I have looked at states that many near-death survivors not only have heightened sensitivity to light and sound but can also have an aversion to red meat. So, too, are there heightened sensations of taste, touch, texture, and smell.

So what does the research say about my snippets of pictures, or pre–déjà vu, that seemed to be causing me so much fear? Many researchers have confirmed that an experiencer of a near-death trauma will have increased intuitive abilities. Atwater (1996) describes the psychic abilities like this:

Extrasensory perception and various types of psychic phenomena become normal and ordinary in the lives of NDErs. A person's religious beliefs do not prevent this expansion of faculties or enlargements of perceptual range. This can frighten the unprepared and be misconstrued as "the devil's work" when it is actually more akin to "gifts of the spirit."

The same message is echoed in other qualified sources. After researching, interviewing, and documenting thousands of near-death experiencers' accounts, IANDS states that an experiencer can have:

... increased intuitive/psychic abilities plus the ability to know or "re-live" the future.... There's no denying that experiencers become quite intuitive afterward. Psychic displays can be commonplace, such as ... "remembering" the future, finishing another's sentence, "hearing" plants and animals "speak." This behaviour is not only worrisome to relatives and friends; it can become frightening to them.

This third party information was a huge source of comfort for me. I loved knowing that I was not alone and that there were other people like me struggling and searching for their *new normal*. Everything that I read told me I was normal under this abnormal circumstance, and that I would remain like this for the rest of my life.

But the question still remained: how was I going to live with this new normal? No matter where I searched, there didn't seem to be an answer as to how to cope. I was told that coping mechanisms vary significantly depending on the emotional stamina of an individual. *If* each day there are more than 750 people in the United States alone surviving a near-death experience, certainly some of them at one point or another would have difficulty coping. Therefore, if science can provide and describe a loosely based psychological and physiological profile of the after-effects of an NDE, then a coping strategy should be relatively simple. Who better to share all her coping strategies than the one who needed it the most—me!

Slowly, my life began to make sense. I understand now that I am not in control, but that I have choices. My snippets of pictures, or pre-déjà vu, haven't gone away, but I have become accustomed to them. I still prefer not to consume red meat, although I can now cook it for my family. We don't go through as many light bulbs as we used to because I have surrendered to my new life. The television remote control, clocks, and phones still act up due to my increased vibrational level, but I am no longer fearful. I still have heightened sensitivity to light and sound, but my husband and I have learned to compromise. Without effort, I automatically feel the *vibrational energy* of everyone but have learned to *shield* myself, allowing me to go into a few more public places.

But most importantly, I discovered a heightened spiritual intuitiveness that allows me to access unfathomable wisdom from many spiritual teachers. I have called these wise teachers my Choir. The wisdom, love, understanding, and knowledge that I've received from this Choir are too incredible and electrifying to keep to myself. Imagine receiving all the answers to any of your questions anytime you want to. Well, now you can! And you will never guess how I stumbled upon them!

* * *

CHAPTER ELEVEN

My Choir

The real voyage of discovery consists of not in seeking
new landscapes but in having new eyes.

~Marcel Proust

The words were deep, loud, and muffled. It sounded as if someone had stuck an empty paper towel tube deep in my ear; it tingled my spine and vibrated my brain. I snapped my head around, expecting to see someone. But nothing! What the hell was that? A hot flash came over my body, giving me goose bumps at the same time.

We had just sold our house and I was busy packing. My mind drifted aimlessly as I wrapped and boxed up the kitchen dishes. This was not a day for *this* nonsense. "If you have something to say ... say it already or get out of my head!" Then the voice was quieter, but still deep within my head. "Oh, for God's sake, I don't have time for this today, leave me alone!" I muttered. And it did.

Periodically I would have the same experience, and each time I couldn't be bothered giving in to this freaky side-effect—until I had another SVT. Because we hadn't quite moved yet, the stress of packing and my fatigue triggered another attack. As I lay on the hospital bed and the medical staff went through their usual routine, I heard the voice again, but this time it was loud, clear, and audible. "*Not this one.*" What the hell did that mean?

As one of the nurses approached my side to administer my IV, I heard the voice say it again, but louder: "NOT THIS ONE." I could hear it perfectly, but I had no idea what it meant. Then I began to panic. The thoughts raced through my mind, "I'm not going to die on *this* SVT?" Is that what it means? Does it mean I'm going to be cardioverted because the medicine won't work? Is that what it means? What the hell does that mean? My panic escalated. I was already in SVT with an incredibly racing heart; *now* was not the time for *any* of this nonsense!

As I mentioned earlier, the IV needle is an 18-gauge, which is the size of a lead pencil and hurts unbelievably when it pierces the vein. As the nurse pierced my vein, blood began pouring down my arm. She then missed the vein and kept stabbing and poking, then stabbing and poking some more. She was moving it around as if she was drawing a picture. The blood was now starting to soak the bed; I was writhing in pain, sweating profusely, AND in an SVT!

"What the hell is going on . . . can't you get it? . . . that hurts . . . what's the problem?" "I'm sorry, you have a lot of scar tissue, and it's a little tricky." Actually, she was a student who probably wasn't used to that much scar tissue. But I was a patient who wasn't used to that big of a *butcher job* with an IV!

But the voice was right: *Not This One.* I will never forget the face of that nursing student, and I will *never* allow her to put another IV into my arm. From that moment on, I was hooked! I listened with great interest; I was intrigued by the profound wisdom and in disbelief that this could even be real. To prove to myself that this *must* be merely my own *subconscious*, I started listening and carefully documenting, which seemed to naturally develop our unique mode of communication.

It became clear that the knowledge I heard couldn't possibly be from me. I'm smart, but *they* are smarter! This was by far the greatest, most supreme, freakiest side-effect of all! And I loved it!

I don't know why or how, but for some reason I can hear what *feels* to me to be *higher vibrational energies*. I communicate with them in exactly the same way I fluidly conveyed thoughts with my dad in that *darkest blackness* that I described earlier. But I want to be clear: when I refer to *hearing* them, it is more like *feeling* or *sensing* what they are saying. I convert what I *feel* into the best words that perfectly suit their message so humans can understand it. Therefore, the usage of words within this book may not be *grammatically correct* or even *dictionary real* or what an English professor would classify as acceptable—because I write what I get!

The words in blocks of *italicized lettering* or any definition in *italicized lettering in {brackets}* are from my Choir. The content may sound choppy or contain very short/long sentences; again, I can only give what I get. For further clarity, I have provided a detailed glossary with numerous words that were either newly created or words that already existed but had a slightly different and unique meaning from what we are used to. This is done because sometimes there are no other words that best describe what needs to be translated.

In the early stages of developing our communication, there were more than five, but fewer than ten, *vibrational energies* to learn from. They all seemed to form a semicircle in front of my mind's eye, just as you would imagine a choir would do. Some of the energies have a *higher vibrational* level than the others. For example, one was very commanding—not mean, just a strong presence—while another was very soft, tender, and gentle. While some can be hard to hear, others are booming loud; but, they are all very loving, kind, and above all, so patient. Normally, only one *vibrational energy* shares at a time, but occasionally many will offer at once. When they are all sharing it can be very overwhelming, hard to tune out, and difficult to distinguish. That is why I call them my Choir.

In the beginning, our conversation was only one-way. They spoke, I listened. As our communication grew I couldn't help but share with my sister what this Choir was telling me. She would ask it questions and I would give her their answer. But it never occurred to me, until months later, that I too could ask my own questions. From that day on, I have been like a giddy schoolgirl with a childhood crush or a kid in the candy store. I have been exploring ever since, and let me tell you, what a screwed-up world we live in! Nevertheless, it has been exhilarating!

Originally, this *communicational gift* started off with one *vibrational energy*, then another and another. I seemed to learn from each one. Each seems to have its own set of gifts. But the strong, commanding *vibrational energy* was always there surrounded by the others. Throughout the development of our communication, one by one, each soft *vibrational energy* became a layer behind the commanding strong one. Although none of them has gone anywhere and I can still access them all, their teachings, wisdom, and guidance now seem to be represented by one.

The Choir is a representation of a collective group of highly vibrational spiritual energies that offer assistance for those who have chosen to listen. The word Choir best represents what I feel, because as each individual singer in a choir makes up one collective unit, their singing is a form of communication and their song is the message. Different songs hold different messages, but the singing never changes. Choirs don't disappear; only their individual members come and go. The group of highly vibrational spiritual energies is similar to all the singers in a choir, their messages are like the songs that we listen to, and receiving their form of communication through *sensing* is similar to hearing the music.

My Choir's messages are incredibly thrilling ... invigorating and too powerful to hoard and keep to myself. The ability to hear them initially caused me horrible fear and anxiety, but now I am so blessed that they never quit singing in my ear! The *gift* is not the ability to hear;

the *gift* is the collective group of highly spiritual vibrational energies. Anyone has the ability to hear if they choose to.

Throughout this book you will get to know the teachings and wisdom of my Choir. You will easily see the difference between my writing capabilities and theirs: I use grammar and punctuation! However, as I share my personal points of view, you will easily recognize my narrowed, naive view in comparison to the wisdom, expansiveness, and loving nature of my Choir's!

I am no different than you. I might have had different experiences that shaped my life and made me who I am today, but I remain the same as you. I am not asking you to believe what I am saying is true, because I cannot ask of you what I couldn't ask of myself. I wasn't able to believe or trust and I used to live in fear and uncertainty ... until now!

But just for fun, aren't you a little bit curious what *your* Choir would sound like? Wouldn't you like to have *all* the answers at *your* fingertips? Would you like to know if there is an afterlife or Heaven? Where is Heaven? Is the afterlife the same as Heaven? Or is all of this stuff just *make-believe* and *imagination* like Santa Claus and the Tooth Fairy?

Well, I am going to give you those answers and show you how to find *your own* Choir, if that is what you want. If you or someone you love is struggling with death and dying, I am going to offer you some peace through answers. If *you* have any fear about death, the afterlife or dying, you will find comfort in the next couple of chapters. Some might be surprised by the answers and comments I've provided, yet some others may be moved by their own stirred emotions. There is something for everyone, I promise.

* * *

CHAPTER TWELVE

Death, Dying, & the Afterlife

Life is pleasant. Death is peaceful.
It's the transition that's troublesome.

~Isaac Asimov

This is a very important chapter. This is the beginning of slowly starting to understand the debilitating effects of fear. Understanding fear is a critical element in *recognizing* what *shouldn't* be in our lives. It was hard for me to write this chapter because the past doesn't exist for me anymore. As soon as the moment slips away, it is as if I'd never remember it. It didn't always used to be like this for me. I used to easily remember the past and how some people in my life, who claimed to love me, had wronged me. Without any effort at all, I could remember all those painful and hurtful situations that I grudgingly kept close to my heart. I would have no trouble reminding other people of those horrible situations and painful events. This only caused more pain and unknowingly fuelled fear's flame. But now, after my NDE, I've written this chapter as a reflection of my past and my current state of *being* and living in a heightened state of consciousness.

* * *

I can admit that before my NDE, I was afraid to die. I would worry about how my family would react and how my passing would cause them tremendous pain. Would I be buried or cremated? I was fearful that I would die without having all the things done on my *bucket list*. I was not ready to go; I still had so much to do and lots to see. What would I do when I got there?

Having been born and raised Catholic, I wondered if Judgment Day was going to be horrible or if Hell really existed. Are there different levels to the spiritual world or is transition of the body only to one level? Often I wondered if there would be a warning signal that my death was imminent and if I would have time to prepare. Would dying be painful or would I be like a ghost and float around watching all my loved ones cry for me? I wondered if the people who have already died would be waiting for me near a beautiful stream, by green grass, with harps playing in the background.

I wondered if Heaven was up in the sky as I was taught as a child. Or was it an adult's easy way out in describing to me where my pet went when it died? I wondered if my loved ones who had passed on could see me. Do they know I miss them? Can they see me when I cry? Is it possible to communicate with the dead? Are there such things as ghosts?

Before I died, I had all of these questions and so many more. Now I am delighted to report that death isn't like anything I could have ever imagined.

What I am about to share with you is based on *my* personal experience since surviving a NDE and living in a higher *vibrational* level.

Death is not a *place* or *a state of being*; it is a process. It is only once you *are dead* that you can feel complete stillness, joy, and peace.

Do we know when we are going to die?

Yes, I believe so. The moment my SVT happened and we were driving to the hospital I knew something was very wrong. What I didn't know, and may never know, is when I actually transitioned. How long was I there? When I was standing with my dad, I didn't have a consciousness of time as we know it. I didn't know that Dad was dead because we were not in the form of a physical body but of a *spiritual vibrational energy.*

Only in our conscious mind do we think in terms of a *body.* When our bodies become old, diseased, or injured, they break down and die. Therefore, when you are no longer in your body, there is no longer any *thinking*, only a *sensing.* You don't <u>know</u> that there is *death* because *you* cannot *identify with your body.*

Another example of knowing when we are about to die involves loved ones who've had a fatal illness and *knew* it was their time. Before my NDE, I had a good friend who was diagnosed with an aggressive cancer. We all knew at some point this horrible disease would take his life.

He was now living permanently at the hospital, where his medication was increased to help him cope with the pain. I had visited him and his wife and was on my way out as more visitors arrived. He was in such good spirits, laughing and joking and craving a cigarette. As I left, he planned to enjoy a cigarette, joking that it really couldn't hurt him anymore, he was already dying!

Apparently, shortly after I left everyone went outside to have a cigarette. It was a beautiful day and everyone was in good spirits and lighthearted. As they were wheeling him back to his room, he panicked, saying, "Stop, something is wrong, I feel different, something is very wrong."

They quickly called for a nearby nurse, but by the time she had reached him, he had already passed on. Therefore based on my experience, yes, I believe we all know when we are going to die. However, each mind does not process that information in the same way; hence, our mind's perception will differ from person to person. When in a fatal situation, you will have an inner knowledge or intuition that something is horribly wrong but you may not necessarily mentally process it by calling it *death.*

Is it painful to die?

Yes and no. I believe it can be physically painful to die. Remember, death is a process; it is a means to an end, not a place. I believe that there may be some pain leading up to it, but at a certain point, in the beginning of ultimate transition, I believe that there is no longer any pain. An example that comes to mind for me is a victim of crime. The media has documented or sensationalized the crimes of murderers and recounted the horrific details of how they had killed their victims.

I used to find those documentaries fascinating, but now I cannot watch them at all. I get anxious and a really sick feeling comes over my body when I think of the final minutes of someone's life who had been brutally killed, murdered, or tortured. I believe that we are all consciously alert and have a *built-in* knowledge about our impending doom or ultimate death. While we may still feel pain and still possess thought, we will have enough alertness to make a decision to surrender to the process of death or fight to stay alive. If the body's injuries are too great to sustain and maintain life, the mind will surrender and the pain will be gone.

However, the survival stories you may have seen on television share how close some people were to death but still had such a great *will* to survive. Some of the stories are truly amazing and defy all odds or reasonable explanations. The survivor's *will to live* was greater than the impulse to surrender to the process of death. I believe this type of *will* to be an alert conscious thought and the reason for their successful survival.

What is death?

It is very frustrating for me now when I hear the word *death*. I feel we have bastardized the word and continue to use it incorrectly. Death is *only* a process leading to something else. It is not a place to go. It is *how* you get there. I believe it is only a process in which our body begins to shut down. It is a process that prepares the body to transition to become nothing more than a shell. The process of shutting the body down can be painful, whether it is through disease, an accident, a heart attack, a drowning, or any violent nature. Or this process can be spiritual, peaceful, and filled with acceptance ... you get to decide.

IMAGINE

> *Think of yourself as an egg. Your body is the shell. The egg yolk is your high vibrational spiritual energy that lives on forever. Some egg shells are decorated prettily, or are old, and some are cracked. We are all eggs. It doesn't matter what your shell looks like; when that shell breaks it will be discarded. It doesn't matter where that shell is put, or how it is discarded. The most important part is the yolk. The shell's only job is to protect the yolk. The yolk never dies. It is all-knowing.*

Are Heaven and the afterlife the same thing?

Being raised a Catholic, and before my NDE, I would have said yes to Heaven and the afterlife being the same thing. But today I would have to say no.

To me, Heaven is Catholic and religious and the afterlife is spiritual. I don't even believe that these two words mean the same thing! Heaven is a place, and the afterlife feels more like a destination. Heaven is a place we all *hope* to go to; it seems conditional and you must qualify for it by being good on earth. But if you weren't good on Earth does our loving Father send his child to Hell? The afterlife is a destination that you *don't* have to qualify for, and you are never threatened with having it taken from you. It's a destination of certainty. No one asks *where* the afterlife is, yet so many people want to know *where* Heaven is. Why?

What we all *really* want to know is whether there is something for us after the body transitions from a shell, and the spirit is left without a home. Do we reunite with our loved ones who previously passed? Do we have a soul or spirit? And to that, my answer is unequivocally Yes!

Does Heaven exist? Is Heaven up in the sky?

Heaven is a magical place of hope that we have created to ease our fears, to keep us good so paradise isn't taken from us, and the thought of Heaven is the building block to teach us faith. If you want to believe that Heaven is up in the sky, or that it looks like the pearly gates with gold-covered roads, harps, and streams, that is okay. The most important aspect is not where it is located, or what it looks like, but rather that you have *faith* that Heaven exists.

The exact location of Heaven doesn't really matter, does it? Know that your beautiful version of Heaven will be waiting for you someday. No matter what vision of Heaven you can create in your wonderful, overactive imagination, Heaven will be more glorious than your mind has the capability of imagining. Trust me—you will not be disappointed.

Regarding the perception of some sort of qualification process, everyone goes to Heaven! *If* you haven't been as good as you would have liked, there is forgiveness. The Divine Source is love and within His Love *is* His forgiveness. This doesn't mean that you have carte blanche to do whatever you want here, but please know that only love exists in Heaven and within love is forgiveness! No matter what you did, you will be forgiven.

But for those of you who are really curious about the location of Heaven, it is my heart and soul's opinion that Heaven is up, and here is why. Anytime we face horrible unexpected emotion and look for quick solace we seem to turn our faces up toward the sky, almost as a knee-jerk reaction. When it is a beautiful day outside we look to the sky and remark on how wonderful it is, while we take in a deep breath of fresh air. When we want to talk to the Divine Source or God, we naturally and without prompting seem to look to the sky.

Heaven's precise location will always remain a mystery, but I know that our bodies are wonderful creations with so many *built in* functions that we can't comprehend them all. So if your body wants to *look up* to find Heaven, God, the Divine Source or the Creator, then that's where it is for you. Just know that Heaven does exist, that it is more beautiful than humanly imaginable, and that Heaven is waiting for everyone ... good or bad.

Why are we scared to die?

For each person it is different, but I believe that there is only one main reason why death is feared. No one has died, gone to Heaven, visited for a while and then brought back a memento to show others. It's not like going to the moon, picking up a rock, and bringing it back to the earth as proof.

There is no proof when we speak of death or the afterlife. A lack of proof is the *basis* for our fear of death. Not *knowing* the *unknown* is behind our fear. There is only one way to eliminate a fear of death, and that is *faith*. It doesn't matter how you find faith or where you find it. Faith is not a religion and it is not found in threats or demands. Faith is love of *Oneness*, which will produce only goodness.

Not everyone is afraid to die. Are you?

* * *

CHAPTER THIRTEEN

Three Reasons We May Fear Death

When the heart weeps for what it has lost,
the soul laughs for what it has found.

~Sufi aphorism

When someone we know is dying, it can be uncomfortably awkward. Conversations can be strained, emotions run high, and our normal behaviour seems to misbehave. To calm our fears surrounding death, we seek out stories of those who have survived a near-death experience. It is in our seeking that our fascination with and curiosity about death comes alive. Sometimes the search soothes our fears and allows us to put many of our frazzled emotions into better perspective, while at other times our fears and insecurities get triggered.

Many people look to the experiences of near-death survivors as proof that an afterlife exists. Their stories provide hope that there is a better place for us when we leave this earth. It is in processing this information that our emotions such as fear can change our perceptions. So throughout this chapter, recognize your thoughts and challenge your perceptions. It is in changing our perceptions that fear can be minimized, if not eliminated.

We all hope that when we die, it is not the end. Here is where organized religion is born. Within the foundation of religion comes a *spiritual knowing* called *faith*. We all have faith. We all need faith. Faith can be found in dogmas, religious rituals, doctrines, or experiences. In some fashion or another, we all have some sort of faith. Many believe in a Higher Power, Creator, or Divine Source. For those who don't believe, they still have faith, but in something else.

The foundation of our faith is a promise of hope that we will be reunited someday with our loved ones who have passed on. Even with faith, there remains no proof of an afterlife; here lies the controversy and our fear.

There is only one main reason why death is feared: it is unknown. The unknown is the basis for all our fears, and for each of us it has three components: (1) fear of *how* I am going to die; (2) fear of *where* I am going; and (3) fear of *leaving* loved ones behind.

Fear of How I am Going to Die. Will it Hurt?

As I freely admitted, before my NDE, I was afraid to die. Now, since my NDE, I can clearly see that most of my fear was born out of the unknown. The unknown can be very frightening, even debilitating. I believe the most fearful component to death is in fearing *how* we are going to die.

Most of my life has been spent in and out of hospitals with my heart arrhythmia. Each time I would have an attack I was continually faced with *how* I would probably die someday, as any one of these attacks could take my life. I had often wondered if it would be quick or painful; would I know or just slip away?

So before I would go to the hospital, I would make sure that my hair was clean and curled, makeup was on, my legs were shaved and I had clean underwear on! After my hundredth attack, I realized that my vanity was silly and that my SVT probably wasn't going to kill me. But the fear still remained: no matter *how* I die, will it hurt?

Let me share something with you. When I was pregnant with my son, I once asked my mom, "How will I know when to push?" With all her wisdom after having six children, she said, "God has it all built in!" Now what the hell kind of an answer is that, I thought. Almost nine months pregnant, fearful about the excruciating pain that my pregnancy books describe, and all she gives me is ... *God has it all built in!*

After my son was born I shared with my mom what pushing was like. I told her, "It's a little like puking, only from the other end!" So now, when I am asked if death is painful, I find myself in my mom's shoes. As with childbirth, I believe that our bodies have many things *built in*, many things that we don't even know about.

Our bodies are spectacular creations. I believe that the human body was created with a kind of *shut off valve* in the brain. In the moment of impending death, a part of our mind shuts off and triggers a *silent knowing* that something is wrong or different. If you are experiencing some pain at that moment, when the *silent knowing* is triggered, your pain will disappear. Whether you fight your situation all the way or surrender to it peacefully, know that the pain will be gone. Our incredible body was created just that way.

I believe this is the first point at which transitioning begins. Speaking only of my experience, I had everything to live for. I wanted to live, I was still very afraid to die. I didn't want to leave my poor young son and new husband to live life without me. But something happened; almost like a click of a switch ... a *silent knowing* ... I was totally at peace and freely accepted my fate. I was no longer in pain, had no thoughts of my family, and my thoughts seemed clearer.

Just before this transitioning point, you might be in some pain. You might know that something just isn't right. You might be thinking of your loved ones or of the regrets you have. Your will to survive might kick in to fight the situation, or you may just surrender peacefully to your circumstances. Then ... *click* ... everything is perfect, peaceful, contently surrendered. You are contentedly right with the world. No matter *how* you go, I believe that you will know and that you will ultimately get to decide. Are you going to fight it all the way or surrender peacefully? The choice is yours and the fear you feel is your own creation.

Fear of the Afterlife or Lack Thereof

Fear of death and the hope of an afterlife constitute the foundation of many organized religions. There are many questions about an afterlife. Is there an afterlife? What do we do there? Does Hell exist? Is there a Judgment Day? If there is an afterlife, will I automatically go there? If I am bad on earth will I go to Heaven? The answers to any of these questions of course cannot be proven.

Many of the suggestions about the possibility of an afterlife have come from religious leaders, spiritual teachers, and those who have undergone a near-death experience. They are all only theories, suggestions, and opinions based on dogmas, experiences, or feelings. Any of your thoughts that an afterlife truly exists or doesn't exist are based solely on your faith, your beliefs, your religious background, and your sense of hope. Obviously no one can prove that an afterlife exists; I can only share with you what I now believe about the afterlife since my NDE and living in a *heightened spiritual vibration.*

Everything we have here on earth is physical. Houses, cars, boats, money, debt, hugs, kisses, tears, sight, hearing, touch, anger, sadness, fear. None of this is there, in the afterlife. No physical properties, no emotions as we know them, no sadness, anger, fear, helplessness, sickness. There are no senses, no touch, no sight, no hearing—only a *knowing.* There is no sense of time such as minutes, seconds, days, just a quiet timelessness of stillness—perfect existence. It is so perfect that you don't want to leave. It is where you are meant to be.

That is why it is so hard to be back here on earth once paradise has been touched. When I tried to describe this to my husband, he asked, "So what do you do ... float around all day?" "No," I quipped, "there is no such thing as a day or floating!" This is a difficult concept to share using words. Our world is strictly physical and most of us live immersed in materialism. The peace I felt was not of this plane, nor was it of the physical mind, and that is why it is so hard to describe. I believe that there are many levels to the afterlife. The little bit that I was privileged to have touched was complete peace and perfect stillness, communication without any effort. Basically, I no longer ask, "*Is there an afterlife?*" but rather, "*How many levels are there to the afterlife?*"

Fear of Parting from Loved Ones and our Possessions

Your mind plays havoc with your fear of leaving your loved ones; this fear is then spun into disastrous perceptions. Change your perception and you will lose the fear. The worry about how your loved ones will carry on or the potential financial burden that dying could cause is only perception and is easily solved.

Many enjoy their life to the fullest and don't want to leave their material possessions such as their nice home, car, boat, or money. This is a fear of loss which perpetuates an uncomfortable uncertainty. When the body starts to transition, your money, cars, houses, worries, fears, and emotional connections to family will cease.

If you are worried about the financial welfare of your family, should something happen to you, take care of it *now* ... then your worry is gone. If you don't have your funeral arrangements made and fear that the burden will be too much for your family, take care of it *now* ... then you won't be so fearful. We fear leaving our loved ones because we are not prepared, so please: get prepared.

Before my experience, I did not have a Last Will and Testament or any funeral arrangements. If something had happened to me, my son and my husband would have been lost. Now, I have a Will, and my funeral arrangements are planned. And I have learned that each time I leave a friend or family member, I kiss and hug them goodbye, as I never know if I will get that chance again.

Before my experience, I did not have any life insurance. Now, out of respect for my family, I will not burden them with the financial pressure that funerals tend to bring. This is no longer a concern for me, and it's well worth those few dollars it costs me each month.

Death and dying is an uncomfortable subject that no one wants to deal with. Dealing with death isn't just physical and financial, it is also emotional. The hardest part of death is the survivors' grief, which could also be another source of fear surrounding death. But you can take care of that too!

After more than 120 SVT episodes, my condition became critical. I was put on a long waiting list for a complicated heart procedure. Then one day, without warning or any preparation, my bed was ready. Because I had no notice to say goodbye, I took precautions and wrote a note to each one of my family members in case I died.

The pain of grief is inescapable. No matter how much you try to escape, how much you spend, how hard you cry, or how much you try to forget, grief never goes away ... you just learn how to live with it.

CHAPTER FOURTEEN

Grief is Real

Death leaves a heartache no one can heal,
love leaves a memory no one can steal.

~Irish Saying

I'm sure you've heard the saying, "Time heals all wounds," and I suppose this is also true for grief. I wanted to share with you my grief and suffering regarding two incredibly important moments in my life. I offer my intimate stories as examples of comparison of my perception before my NDE and after. I do this only to illustrate what a *spiritual vibrational shift* looks like. Grief is intimate and personal, and there is no right or wrong, just what is.

* * *

My first personal experience with death was when I was twenty-one years old. I was already living on my own when I was seriously traumatized watching my grandmother pass away. My dad called all of us kids to let us know that she was very sick and probably *not going to make it*. I rushed to the hospital, where I was joined by other family members.

By the time I got to my grandmother's side she was already in a coma, but the nurses said she could still hear us. I wondered if this was true. I was shocked by what I saw. This vibrant, feisty little Ukrainian woman was now frail, lying lifeless and breathing very shallowly with long pauses between each breath. I was filled with so much regret and deep sadness. I nestled close to her and I sobbingly whispered in her ear that I was sorry that I hadn't spent more time with her. I begged her to please open her eyes so I could see her and hear her voice just one more time.

I begged her for forgiveness and told her how much I loved her. Although my world was in chaos and complete despair, my grandmother looked like she was at peace. Everyone was so sad and in utter disbelief that the matriarch of this family was now slipping away. The painful helplessness of not being able to do anything was on everyone's face. Although she was still warm to touch, everything else seemed so cold.

For several hours we all took turns at her bedside making sure she was never alone. We all aimlessly waited around for hours. I would go from my grandmother's room, to the hallway, then to the *family room*. This was a segregated private room that a hospital provides for situations like this.

I felt useless. I did not know what I should be doing. It felt weird milling around waiting for someone to die. It just didn't seem right to me; there must be something I should be doing.

I couldn't seem to comfort anyone and no one could really comfort me. It felt more like a holding pattern, filled with shock, grief, and a wondering curiosity about what was about to happen. As I walked around in shock to think this was even happening, I made one of my passes back to my grandmother's room. I noticed that her children, my aunts and uncles, were all at her bedside. There was no longer a place to sit so I stood at the foot of her hospital bed. There were long gaps between each one of her breaths. As my grandmother breathed slowly out, she never took in another breath.

Seconds turned into minutes with no return breath. I didn't know what I was seeing; I couldn't believe this was happening. I anxiously waited for what was normal: another breath. But it didn't come. It might have only been a couple of minutes but it felt like forever. The deadening silence was broken by my uncle screaming, "Mom!" This scared me terribly. My poor grandmother horribly gasped in her last breath. The heart monitor that she was on no longer registered any waves; it was just a flat line. My grandmother's only daughter sobbed uncontrollably. Her grief was inconsolable and devastating to watch.

For the first time in my life, with my grandmother's passing, I realized that life is very fragile. It can be taken away from you in a heartbeat. I learned that watching a loved one slip from a warm body to a cold shell is called death. I learned that death was traumatizing and not something that I ever wanted to witness again. I learned quickly that the pain of grief is real and potentially disabling. Death is not only a process but it is also unpredictable. It was the unpredictability of life that I began to fear.

At the time of my grandmother's passing, and being twenty-one years old, I learned two huge lessons. First, we are only carcasses. When the carcass stops working its energy must go somewhere. We need to take care of our carcasses because if we don't we will die; and we can die at any time. Secondly, living with guilt and regrets are two of the most painful components of grief; and if grief could buckle my strong aunt, I could only imagine what it would do to me if I lost one of my parents.

In those two lessons, I learned at an early age that death causes horrible pain. My yappy mindless perception began to fear death, questioned whether the body *does* have energy within it; if it does exist, where does it go? I obsessively took care of my body for fear it would fail me and I too would die, challenging my own mortality. I became paralyzed with fear that life was so unpredictable, not only for me but for all those that I loved and needed around me; a huge sense of insecurity grew within. My guilt and regret anchored me in the past, preventing me from healing my wound of grief.

After my NDE, and living within a higher spiritual vibrational level, I have a totally different outlook. Yes, it is true that life as we know it *is* unpredictable. The people in your life *could* be taken from you in an instant. But if you live your life in each moment of each day and everyone that you come in contact with is cherished and loved to your fullest, then regrets will not exist.

Understanding that death is a process, not a place to be, fosters a *knowing* that reuniting with loved ones who have transitioned is a certainty. Although the pain of grief is real, increasing your own *vibrational energy* will enable you to feel the energy of your loved ones long after they are gone. It is realizing that the body is the only part that doesn't survive transition, and accepting that *spiritual vibrational energy* is real and within each of us, creates faith. It is in faith that there is forgiveness, love, peace, and patience. It is in living in each moment that you can peacefully settle into a *new normal* without this loved one in your physical world.

I no longer fear the unpredictability of life but embrace it. I spend each day as if it is my last. I don't regret anything. I believe that no matter what situation is thrown at me, it is only temporary and will work itself out in its perfect divine order. I know that we all come from a Divine Source and are created equally. I am in awe at the spectacular creation of our bodies. I have more respect for the body and no longer refer to it as a carcass but as a shell. I have a deep gratitude for all of my experiences from which I was able to learn. Most importantly, death is not traumatizing but a process toward peace. Death is not painful; grief is.

Almost twenty years after my grandmother died, I was in my forties with years of wisdom behind me. It was before my NDE, in April 2008, when my dad, whom I was very close with, lay dying in hospice. I was at my dad's bedside almost every day, sacrificing my job, not spending any time with my son or husband and having little regard for my own deteriorating health. I was overwhelmed with sadness and constantly worried about how I would live life when my dad finally died, and how my son, who was also very close to his *Gedo,* would take his death.

In the last days that I spent with my dad, he was mostly sedated, which gave me many hours to ponder a future without him. I spent hours in quiet solitude surrounded by death in a hospice unit. Many times I prayed to hear my dad's voice just one more time. Often I thought I would hear my dad say something, but it was only my wishful thinking, exhaustion, and my imagination playing tricks on me.

Unlike with my grandmother, I didn't have any regrets with my dad. I had a wonderful relationship with him. I knew that I would greatly miss his company, his advice, his friendship, and the laughter we had shared. As I sat by his bedside, I needed to find some sense of comfort; this great loss needed to have meaning. I coped by convincing myself that this was no life for him and that death would be a blessing for him. But my personal, utter sadness and fear of losing him to the finality of death and never being able to see, touch, or hear him again would still creep in and wreak havoc in my mind.

It was a beautiful morning on Friday, April 25, 2008. Again, I went early to hospice to spend the day with Dad. It was around 8:30 in the morning when I walked into his room. I greeted him as I had every other morning: "Hey You! How are you doing today?" I opened the blinds and got ready to take on yet another day. As with every other day, Dad was heavily sedated and not responsive. I went to the bathroom in my dad's room to wash my apple, which was going to be my breakfast.

As I was coming out of the bathroom my dad opened his eyes and said, "Hello!" I could hardly believe my eyes! I had spent so much time with my sedated father that I thought I was hallucinating. My father was conscious, talking, and smiling. I aggressively rang the emergency button for the nurse and screamed out into the hallway so she could see what I was seeing.

I said, "Dad, I miss you so much: I have so much to tell you." He spoke so clearly, with no evidence that he had had a stroke. He said that he was having incredible dreams and asked me if I thought they meant anything. I told him that it was probably the drugs they had him on. He wasn't in any pain and quite happy to be awake.

I asked, "Did you know that I have been by your bedside?"

"No," he responded.

"Did you hear me talk to you or sing to you?"

"No," he said. I then asked if he knew that his parish priest had come by to say the Last Rites Blessing for him; again he didn't know, but he was grateful. As the nurse was listening to our conversation, she began preparing to give him more sedation. I quickly stopped her, begging and pleading for just a few more minutes with him.

As I lay in my dad's arms, he was running his fingers through my hair telling me how much he loved me. He was reassuring me that everything was going to be okay. Although a grown woman, I felt like his little girl again. I prayed that I would never forget this moment. I knew it was probably going to be my last with him. I wanted it to last forever. Time stood still in that moment, nothing else mattered.

Within a few short minutes my dad lay heavily sedated and I was never to see his eyes or hear his voice again. I sobbed almost that entire day, waiting and hoping for one more stolen moment. Later that same afternoon, my aunt came to visit Dad and had an experience similar to mine, where he was conscious, smiling, and awake. She too was both overjoyed and crushed at having such a fleeting moment and wished that it could have lasted longer. I spent the better part of the next day with Dad, hoping for one more second of alertness.

Late that afternoon, Dad's body started shutting down; at 3:40 a.m. on Sunday, April 27, 2008, he passed away peacefully. My soul-sister Veronica and I were at his bedside as he took his last breath, and I said a prayer that he might find his way to Heaven. I thanked Dad for being the best father he knew how to be. I knew my life would never be the same again and that this heartbreaking sadness probably would never leave me.

My father's death reinforced the importance of living in the moment. The indescribable pain I felt in losing his company made me realize that grief is not only of the mind but also of the body. My physical body ached to hug my dad. I craved seeing his face and hearing his voice one more time. Losing the ability to share anything more with him totally devastated me. How would I live life without him?

The process of my dad's death taught me about miracles. When we think of miracles we have this expectation that they must be grand. If it isn't grand then it's not a miracle. I believe I was blessed with a miracle to see my dad alive one more time. I am grateful that my aunt was also shown the same miracle.

His death also taught me about the rituals of death, such as blessings, graveyards, tombstones, funerals, and prayer services. I was in such despair and nothing seemed to help. Again, being raised Catholic I wondered why none of this was helping my sadness. Although I had faith in a Higher Power and had the hope of Heaven, I was overcome with sadness. I missed him dearly, and the only thing that seemed to help was *time*. I got myself so busy with a huge list of goals and challenges that kept me from feeling any pain. I sold my real estate brokerage, got back into selling, wrote over thirty real estate e-books and created a real estate website called *Soldplicity*. Basically, I did everything I could to *not* live *in the moment* for fear of feeling that gut-wrenching pain and agony of losing Dad.

Two years after my father died and before my NDE, I accepted the fact that he was gone and that I had to surrender to a new season of life with him not in it. I still missed him terribly, but time has a way of healing some wounds. There were days when the pain of his death felt raw, as if it had happened only yesterday, while at other times it felt as if he had almost been a dream and that he had never existed in my lifetime.

After my NDE, I can honestly tell you that the real pain of death is our grief. The ones who get left behind are the only ones floundering. The grief-free moments are found *only* when living *in the moment*. When our loved ones are gone, they don't cry for us, or see us as we see ourselves. Heaven or the afterlife has no comprehension of cruelty— only peace, love, and easy, fluid communication with loved ones.

I understand the physical, emotional, and spiritual pain of grief when losing someone close. The grief I had once felt is now gone.

My perception of death has changed, and automatically so too has my grieving process. I do not think of death as the end but rather as a *transition*. Time heals the painful wound of grief, but grief never goes away, it just gets easier to look at. As our loved one transitions into peace, so too must we. Our transition process is of our mind, with *time* assisting.

When I meet someone who has experienced a huge loss, I explain my kettle theory as reassurance. My *kettle theory* is simple. When we boil water in a kettle, some of the water will evaporate. It doesn't mean that the water is gone; it just means that the water has taken on a different form. Most of us already understand and accept this common scientific fact. Our bodies are much like water. As the water heats up, it goes from a liquid to a vapour. So do our bodies. We transition from a *solid human being* to a *vibrational spiritual being*. That is why when we are *in the moment*, we can feel our loved ones when they are no longer with us. They may be physically gone, but a piece of their *vibrational energy* remains.

So please take some solace in the realization that death is not the end and that death doesn't have to be fearful; we make it scary. Understand that your body is only your shell and not the true *spiritual vibration* that comprises who you really are. Find comfort knowing that the transition to death is not going to hurt and no matter how small or insignificant, miracles can and do happen. It is our perception of miracles that needs to change. And lastly, but just as important, please know that the fact that we can't see our loved ones any longer doesn't mean that they aren't here. We just need to *relearn* how to increase our own *vibrational level* so we can communicate with them again.

Each day we are all transitioning, growing, learning, changing, and evolving. Without death we would not have life; without darkness we would not have light. So if you're ready, it's time to show you *how* to raise your own *vibrational energy*! It is in becoming more individually aware that your life will take on a different meaning, benefiting not only you and those around you, but all of mankind!

* * *

CHAPTER FIFTEEN

Putting It All Together

Learn as if you were going to live forever.
Live as if you were going to die tomorrow.

~Mahatma Gandhi

As I have opened my heart to you and shared my personal NDE, I will continue to give you all that is within me. There are three reasons why I have written and shared my immensely painful journey. First, to justify the amount of pain I suffered; there must be a reason and a purpose for its existence. Second, I wanted to illustrate that I am no different than you, capable of the same feelings and sharing the same strengths and weaknesses. Further, if I can raise my own vibrational level, enjoy spiritual intuitiveness, and live in each moment, I can help you to do the same. Last, but most importantly, I have freely exposed my heart and soul to you with the hope that you can be as brutally honest with *yourself.* It will only be with authentic honesty that any change can occur within us.

For the remainder of this book, my NDE will *only* be used as an example to illustrate lessons or teachings. It is *not* intended, nor will it be used, to separate you from me. Other than our personal experiences, there is no difference between us. **This is *Oneness.***

It doesn't matter if you believe that the beginning of your creation was through the ashes of divine creation, evolution, or the Big Bang Theory. What matters is that *you* were *created* by a *source*. The passionate debates that are fuelled over *how* you were created really don't matter here. What truly matters is that *you exist* and that *the same source* that made you, made me too! Therefore, you and I share the same source.

Although we share the same source, the label of that source will depend on your beliefs, childhood rearing rituals, your personal experiences, etc. Some of us will call it a Higher Power, God, Lord, Universe, Creator, Almighty Power, Jesus, etc. To spare us an argument or debate, I have labelled this Source as the ***Divine Source.*** The label is not important; understanding the lessons and teachings are.

My NDE showed me that, as humans, we are made up of two parts. The first part is our body. Our body is the only part that is capable of dying or the process of transition. The body is what our five human senses grieve when a loved one is gone. We miss the smell of their cologne or perfume, the sight of their face, the sound of their voice and laughter, the touch of their skin, and the taste of their kisses.

Our second part, which again is often subject to heated debates because it can't be proven, is our body which has an *energy* contained within it. How do I know this? Because it was this energy that I felt during and after my NDE. This *energy*, whether you **choose** to *know* it or *feel* it, is *always* directly connected to our Divine Source and automatically accessible at anytime. This *energy* can be felt. It's like *vibration.* This *energy* or *vibration* is what some might call a *spirit* or a *soul.*

For the remainder of this book, the second part of a human being that might also be known as our soul or spirit will be referred to as the ***spiritual vibrational energy.*** *Our spiritual vibrational energy* never dies and is a reflection of *our* true essence.

Therefore, as humans we are made up of two parts: the body that man can reproduce through procreation, and the *spiritual vibrational energy* that we got from our *Divine Source*. Children have very high *spiritual vibrational energies*. This is not to be confused with their innocence. It is the children's innocence that allows them to remain in a high *spiritual vibrational energy* level, because they don't know any differently. As children grow, the harsh and cruel realities of life slowly rob them of innocence. In the process, their connection to the Divine Source becomes distant and clouded.

The purpose of this book is to help you relearn what you already know and re-strengthen your connection to the Divine Source. The process is very simple because the connection was never lost.

You might be asking yourself right now, *how* does she plan to do this? As I promised in the beginning, I am going to share with you a simple universal process that, unknowingly, my painful journal entries depicted. It is through this process that you will be jolted with such a huge natural shift in your thinking that it will automatically reopen and immediately reconnect to the Divine Source. This huge natural shift in thinking is called a **spiritual vibrational shift**. A spiritual vibrational shift is {*anything that causes or makes to cause a re-closeness, reuniting, reconnectivity back to the Divine Source from once you were*}.

A *spiritual vibrational shift causes* you to experience spiritual intuitiveness, heightened vibrational levels, and psychic awareness. Being in this state of higher consciousness or awakening is called being in **spiritual consciousness.** *Spiritual consciousness* is a unique state of living. It allows you to be in the moment, fully aware with your senses highly acute, and your intuition peaking. In this consciousness, you are able to experience incredible visions, divine wisdom, knowledge, and surreal peace. *Spiritual consciousness* is a human state of living and *being*. It does not exist in death, and it exists only on this earthly plane. *Spiritual consciousness* is taught by spiritual leaders.

So, basically, this book was written to *inform* you about the existence of *spiritual vibrational shifts*. That is very simple. You are already connected to the Divine Source, you have enough struggles each day that are perfect for practicing on, you are already connected to Oneness, which means you know what to do! You've just forgotten ... and I am here to refresh your memory!

It's very simple. Trauma; Struggle; Search for Relief; Shift; Peace or Resolution! First you experience a Trauma of some sort; then you Struggle to find normalcy; you Search for relief; recognize the Shift and get relief; find Resolution to trauma or problem.

Problems or traumas occur all the time in our lives. The seriousness of a Struggle will be gauged by your own level of emotional upheaval. A Search process will follow as you frantically try to find some Relief. If Relief is found then there will be a Shift in your thinking and behaviour. The Shift will bring Resolution. If you do not have a Shift, you will not find Relief or peaceful Resolution! When people do not know how to find the Shift, they will stay stuck in emotional pain!

Once you have mastered and learned how to obtain a *spiritual vibrational shift* within all your painful emotional situations, you will have mastered *spiritual consciousness*. Once you've received spiritual consciousness you will knowingly be reconnected to the Divine Source. Your vibrational level will be automatically increased. You will automatically obtain spiritual intuitiveness–awakening–and will enjoy psychic awareness. **It is by being connected** to the Divine Source that you will no longer feel grief, fear, anxiety, or worry. Your new life's purpose will reveal itself and the direction of your life will be toward prosperity, happiness, and incredible relationships!

So how do you teach Shift? A Shift is taught through recognition: recognition of love, behaviour, attitude, emotions, thoughts, beliefs, etc. Therefore, this book has only one purpose, and that is to *teach* you *how to find* and *recognize* what a *spiritual vibrational shift* is.

When I share my story with people, they are usually intrigued and want to know *how to find* what I have found. There are only two things holding them back from obtaining exactly what I have: fear and/or lack of motivation. The fear is of letting go of their perceptions. Many people fear that if they become *spiritually conscious* they will *not* be able to do business in a dog-eat-dog world. You can be *spiritually conscious* and still do business; you will just be more successful. Some people fear that if they become *spiritually conscious* the change will be so great that people around them will leave. Actually, it is just the opposite! More people will crave being within your energy and will want to be around you. Your faltering relationships will not dissolve but will become strengthened and imbued with respect. The second thing that holds people back from being *spiritually conscious* is the lack of motivation. Plainly and simply, most people are lazy.

Spiritually conscious is how we were created to be. Although you may conduct yourself differently, your life will become easier, you will be happier, and all those around you will appreciate the change. How do I know all this? Because these were all my fears, and all that *you* question, *I* have questioned too. Throughout this journey I will give you my highest truth and ask of you *only* what I have asked of myself.

Many times I am asked, "Can I find *spiritual consciousness* without having a near-death experience?" And the answer is yes, absolutely. It doesn't matter *what* triggers the search, what's important is your *motivation* behind the Search. Motivation will dictate your success in finding a *spiritual vibrational shift*. For example, my near-death experience was my Trauma. The Struggle was my after-effects. My Search was to eliminate my fear. Although my Search was to eliminate fear, I was passionately motivated to abolish the pain, anger, frustration, loneliness, isolation, depression, bitterness, and guilt *behind* that fear. The *spiritual vibrational shift* came when I embraced and celebrated my new normal. Now I am in Peace and Resolution in spiritual consciousness! It's not your painful or traumatic individual experiences that matter. It is your motivation for your Search and whether you *recognize,* a *spiritual vibrational shift*.

Spiritual consciousness is of the Divine Source which is a part of us;

therefore, we too are part of a Divine Source. We are all-knowing and loving and capable of unfathomable wisdom. We just need to know how to tap into what is already there and has been there from the moment we were conceived. *Spiritual consciousness* is within you and it is your birthright to enjoy. It may be missing right now, but it is certainly not gone. I am honoured to be sharing this journey with you now.

My name is Lorri Brewer, I was born on March 24 and I died on September 19, 2010. I am a highly vibrational spiritual energy, living in spiritual consciousness, and I will be one of your teachers today!

PART TWO

2

The Shift

CHAPTER ONE

The Big Picture

*L*et me begin by introducing myself. Although I will refer to myself as your "teacher," I cannot *teach* you what you *already* know. Therefore, think of me as your *mentor*, merely *reminding* you of what you have *forgotten*. Through our Divine Source, I am connected to you, sharing *Oneness* with you. I am your equal, no better, no worse. Therefore, in a sense, I am also your sister.

The insights in this book were accessed from a highly spiritual point of view that contemplates religion, science, and spirituality. In the first part of this book, "The Journey," I hope that you were able to feel my pain and my honesty, and recognize that I am really just the same as you. Now, as we begin the second part of our journey together, your mind *should* be yearning to learn something. In this part of the book we will switch from *feeling* to *thinking*. We transition from emotion to logic, from listening to *doing*.

Now that you've finished reading and *feeling* my journey in Part One, *your* spiritual awakening, without your even knowing it, has already begun! It's that easy. In this second part, called "The Shift," you will learn from *my* pain, not yours! My NDE is used *only* as an example to illustrate important teachings and will help you understand critical learning lessons. Learning these lessons will require *your* time, patience, and practice. In teaching these lessons I am only *reminding* you of that which you have forgotten. The writing technique of *recapping* will help eliminate any frustration you might encounter as you begin to learn. I have kept the recapping down to a minimum so it isn't annoyingly repetitive, but helpful.

So what is this book about? This book is about *only* one thing, and that is explaining what a *spiritual vibrational shift* is. I will function as your *spiritually conscious mentor*, using my NDE as an illustration of *what* a *spiritual vibrational shift* is.

What *is* a spiritual vibrational shift? It is a natural shift in your *human thinking*, a shift that occurs when you retrain your conscious mind. It is a change in your perception; it is a shift in *conscious knowing*. This is a shift into **knowing** *when* you are *recognizing* **what** needs to be *recognized*.

When this happens—and it will happen, I guarantee it—there will be an automatic and immediate reconnection to the Divine Source. It is a very simple process—*we* are the ones who make it hard!

Just a reminder, the definition of a spiritual vibrational shift is {*anything that causes or makes to cause a re-closeness, reuniting, reconnectivity back to the Divine Source wherein once you were*}.

How am I going to learn this shift? You will learn about, and master practicing, a *spiritual vibrational shift* through a process of **recognition**. When I teach you *how* to *recognize what needs to be recognized*, then you will experience a *spiritual vibrational shift* within your life. It was *this* process that I stumbled upon while trying to recover from the after-effects of an NDE. As your mentor, your equal, your sister, and friend, I will *help you*, but I can't *do* it for you. *All* that you need to learn I will teach you and *all* that you need to remember I will remind you about.

Why is it important to learn about spiritual vibrational shifts? When you learn *how* to experience a *spiritual vibrational shift* within all your painful emotional situations, *then* you will have mastered *spiritual consciousness*.

It is only when you are in <u>*spiritual consciousness*</u> that you will be reconnected to the *Divine Source*. Your vibrational level will be automatically increased and you will automatically obtain spiritual intuitiveness, a higher consciousness, psychic awareness, and an awakening.

When you are *consciously* connected to the Divine Source, you will no longer feel grief, fear, anxiety, or worry. Your new life's purpose will automatically appear, and the direction of your life will be what you have manifested. Your life will be bountiful, filled with beauty, prosperity, happiness, and incredible relationships!

What do I have to do? How long will this take? It does take some effort on your part. The learning process requires your patience. However, feeling a *spiritual vibrational shift* can be obtained very quickly and felt immediately. I promise! I can also guarantee that you've *already* experienced *many* spiritual vibrational shifts in your life. But, you missed *only* one very small step! You missed the part where you *recognized* that you had a *spiritual vibrational shift*. It's that simple.

* * *

As your *spiritually conscious mentor,* I am making *no* demands *of* you, nor do I have *any* expectations *for* you, but I do have *hope* that you will raise your vibrational energy and enjoy an awakening of your own. The trauma of my NDE was an emotionally painful journey, but the rewards of living in *spiritual consciousness* are ineffable and unimaginable. My journey still continues as I have not yet reached my destination.

I am honoured to be your mentor and instructor and I am delighted that my new journey is with you. On our journey together, I am going to show you the **process** of *recognizing what needs to be recognized.* However, I do not teach alone; I have help. I have the assistance of my Choir. Without them this process would be very difficult to explain and even more difficult to understand.

Understanding and learning *spiritual consciousness* is very *simple*; it already *exists* within you, and it is the birthright of everyone. However, *reminding* you of what you already possess can be difficult. With the help of my Choir, and their incredible explanations and reflective insights, explaining *spiritual consciousness* just got easier. Unknowingly, you will also appreciate this additional help.

As your mentor, friend, sister, and instructor, let me share with you that you are exactly where you are meant to be. If you weren't, then this book wouldn't have found you. At this very moment in time, while I have you in *my classroom*, I promise to give you *all* that I have within me. You will receive my highest degree of truth, devotion, and honesty. In return, I ask nothing of you. This now becomes *your* journey and you get to decide what is best for you.

The effort you put into learning will dictate *your* success. You need to decide if you are going to make this process fun or boring, easy or hard, joyful or painful. As Socrates once said, "I cannot teach anybody anything, I can only make them think." Thank you for allowing me this opportunity to make you think; thank you for joining me in *my classroom of life*, and thank you for being my student. And I wholeheartedly thank you for showing me what is to be *my* new journey!

In preparation for the remainder of this book as my student, please treat yourself with care as we go through this process. Give yourself the love, kindness, patience, and respect that are needed when you are spiritually growing. Please remember that learning takes time; it is the *spiritual journey* we need to celebrate, not the destination. Even with the transition of death, our journey never ends.

CHAPTER TWO

Divine Source

The debate about creation is fuelled by different spiritual philosophies, scientific advances, and religious dogmas. No one can say for sure, scientifically, religiously, or spiritually, where we came from. Is there one Supreme Being who created *all* from the ashes and the dust? Or was it organisms in spontaneous generation? Or from the Big Bang theory? No one knows. So why can't we all agree that this debate will remain unanswered until further notice or explanation? I will tell you why: because we *all* want to know if there is a Higher Power, Supreme Being, Almighty Force, or Creator of the Universe. We want answers.

While I do not have all of the answers, I do have what I think is a powerfully compelling *opinion* about *our creation* and the *existence* of a Divine Source. It is an explanation that will make sense and will resonate with your logic, emotion, and spirit. Again, I am not here to debate this point but to share my opinion. If it were up to me, this fruitless debate would be adjourned so we could focus on what is truly important: living life in *spiritual consciousness. But* because this debate exists, let me start at the beginning. We *do not* know *how* human beings were *created*, but we *know* that *whatever* created you, also created me.

Further, *whatever* created you and me remains a mystery. There are so many mysteries within our universe that we may never know them all! That is how vast our universe is. Let's *just pretend* for a moment that evolution *was* responsible for our creation. Then that would mean that there is no Higher Power, no afterlife or Heaven, no proven psychic abilities, no such thing as NDE, no spirits, no angels, and NO faith. How <u>could</u> there be faith if none of this ever existed? We would *know instinctively* that when we died that it was the end with nothing more to follow. So, scientifically, what they call *faith* is actually false hope or wishful thinking.

But we do have faith, we all have faith, we just have *faith* in different things. And we are a creation of supreme intelligence. We also have miracles and vast unknown mysteries of the universe. With the superior intellect of man, coupled with the advances of modern science, many of the world's mysteries have been uncovered. Science has already figured out how to send a man to the moon; find a cure for some cancers; do delicate organ transplants from an animal to a human; perform genetic cloning; make blind people see; and grow babies in test tubes ... but scientists can't figure out *how* we were created? C'mon, really?

What I *do know,* is that *if* we were supposed to *know* how we were created, it probably would have shown itself to us by now, don't you think? There are far too many unanswered mysteries for us to *dismiss* the possibility that a Higher Power *does exist*; there are too many miracles that display the *possible existence* of a Higher Power. Speaking from experience and having done extensive research on NDE, I think the *possibility* of a One Supreme Being is mind blowing! There are thousands of NDE survivors all over the world who report the *knowing* or *intuition* of a Higher Power. They can't all be wrong!

So without a doubt in my mind, we did not evolve from an ape. We are all created equally by *only* One Divine Source, One Supreme Being. This Divine Source is *all*-knowing and responsible for *all* of creation. No doubt about it!

When I say that *we* were *all* created equally by a Divine Source, I mean the *entire universe*; plants, animals, fish, birds and any other existence beyond comprehension. To me the Divine Source is all-encompassing, all-knowing, all-loving, all-wise, and all-forgiving. As a child shares the genes of each parent, so too do we *share* as extensions of the Divine Source in the same all-knowing, all-loving, all-wise, and all-forgiving qualities; we are connected like siblings to *everything else* in existence.

This *connectivity {the actions of connecting; the activity of connecting; methods of coming together; One into/unto them all; All into/unto the One}* of all the elements of our universe to each other, and as an *extension* of *our* Divine Source, is what I mean by **Oneness**. And what you do or don't do affects *Oneness*. Although we represent ourselves as individuals, we present ourselves as One, in much the same way as my Choir does for me. So when my vibrational energy is very low or extremely high, I affect the collective vibrational energy of Oneness. Collectively, the higher the vibrational level, the better it is for all of mankind.

The *Source of Oneness* is *{the source from which all share; collectively equal and a part of; sharing equal and part of One}*. The point is that the Source that made you and me made us all equally as an extension of One Supreme Being. That is why when we are created by and connected to only One Higher Being; it doesn't matter *what* you call *It*.

Whatever perception you have of *your* Higher Power, just know that the One Supreme Being is responsible for your creation and that the creation of Oneness is more than you can imagine. This *Source of Oneness* is supreme greatness, filled with love beyond comprehension, wiser than our vast universe. No matter what you have labelled *It*, we will always remain connected to the same *Source of Oneness*. No matter how great you perceive *It*, it is far more divine than imaginably possible. For the remainder of this book, *our* same *Source of Oneness* or One Supreme Being will be called our **Divine Source**.

Spiritually, we are connected to all other universal beings; this is *Oneness*. It is through our individual faith that we learn to stay in *Oneness*.

As human beings we were all created equally by *only one* Divine Source; a Divine Source of Supreme Being. In other words, we are *a chip off the old block*! We are as the Divine Source made us; we share in the same energy as our Divine Source. And we were created as a combination of two parts: energy and physical. Our energy came from our Divine Source and our physical form came from man through reproduction.

* * *

CHAPTER THREE

Spiritual Vibrational Energy

My NDE showed me that there are two parts to a *human being*. First and foremost, we are energy from our Divine Source, and only then, secondarily, we are a physical form called a body. It is the energy from our Divine Source within us that we call our spirit, our soul, or our spiritual energy. For the remainder of the book, the energy from our Divine Source that is contained within, I have called **spiritual vibrational energy**. This concept too has seen its fair share of debates. I believe we were created equally through the power and love of the same Divine Source creating Oneness within our universe. Hopefully at this point what I am sharing is resonating with you or mirroring some of your own personal beliefs.

As you read in Part One, it was my *spiritual vibrational energy* that left my body and communicated with my dad. After my NDE it was this same part that allowed me to feel the unfathomable wisdom and love of other higher *spiritual vibrational energies*. So, there is no doubt in my mind that we all have a *spiritual vibrational energy* within us!

Let me explain why I think the words *spiritual vibrational energy* best represent what I *know* or *feel* our *spirit* or *soul* is. I love the combination of the words *spiritual vibrational energy*: to me, *spiritual* means not of physical form—invisible and created by a Higher Power; *vibrational* means that we can *all* feel it equally and its strength is capable of being raised or lowered; *energy* means an extension of all that comes from our Divine Source, such as the wisdom, love, and Oneness.

The *spiritual vibrational energy* within us is very powerful, contains unfathomable wisdom, love and forgiveness, and has the ability to fluctuate its energy levels. Our *spiritual vibrational energy* is an extension of, and is always connected to, our Divine Source. It is accessible at any time. It is this *energy* of the *spiritual vibrational energy* that we feel when our loved ones transition to death; not merely our imaginations, as we are told.

Whether you *choose* to *know* it or *feel* it, our *spiritual vibrational energy* has been with us from the moment we were conceived. Everyone's *spiritual vibrational energy* is unique to them; the energy vibrates at different levels at different times. For example, if your *spiritual vibrational energy level* is vibrating particularly high at a given moment, you are able to feel intuitive, have profound thoughts or perceive a déjà vu. This is the same with everyone.

Because we are all connected to Oneness, if you surround yourself with someone who has a particularly high *spiritual vibrational energy* level, in turn, yours will automatically increase. You may not know it at the time, but you will know it when you leave that high vibrational energy level. You will not be as happy, your *spiritual vibrational energy* level will drop, and you will want to get back in touch with that other person.

When a child is born, their *spiritual vibrational energy* level is very high. As the child grows and becomes an adult, the cruelties of life's circumstances lower and dim their *spiritual vibrational energy* level. This is not to say that the connection to our Divine Source has diminished in any way. In fact, the divine connection gets stronger, but we are so backed up and dimmed that we can no longer feel it.

As an analogy, imagine the Divine Source is a permanently open faucet. The clean, sparkling warm water gushing into a sink is the Divine Source's wisdom, love, and knowledge. Your body (life) is the bright, shiny, clean sink. Directly connected to your beautiful sink is a drain, which for this analogy is your *spiritual vibrational energy*. The open faucet, the water, the sink, and the drain are all connected. Therefore, the drain, sink, water, and the faucet are Oneness.

The faucet gushes sparkling clean water into the sink, and *if* the drain is clear of any debris, your sink will remain clean, flow freely, and be bright, and shiny. Said another way, when the faucet of the Divine Source gushes sparkling clean water of love, wisdom, and knowledge into your sink (body-life), and *if* your drain (spiritual vibrational energy) is clear of any debris, your sink will be clean, flowing freely, shiny and bright.

However, if your drain slowly starts to become plugged, the flow of water from the faucet doesn't stop; it never stops. Your plugged drain will prevent your sink from emptying any pooled—and now dirty, stinky—water of pain, debt, anger, hostility, illness, and grudges. Your sink will eventually become full and out of control; it is *only when* it's out of control, stinking, and overflowing that we realize that our sink isn't functioning anymore. We don't know how we got to this point. We don't know *what* we should do about it, but we *know* we *must do* something.

But if you *recognize* that you have a plugged drain, and you knowingly begin to slowly remove each piece of debris, then the beautiful, crystal clear water can flow again. The sink will *automatically* drain, and a plenitude of fresh water will flow, dissolving any memory that your sink was ever plugged. It is in *recognizing* and removing the *debris* that *caused* the *plug* that you will enjoy a beautiful sink again—like you once had—like we once knew. Once you recognize debris, you will never have a plugged drain again; your sink will always remain shiny and new.

The purpose of this analogy is to show you that we all get plugged at one time or another. We all forget what we once were. We forget what an empty, shiny, beautiful sink looks like, and we don't remember where the drain is. We don't know how to unplug the drain. But we all want our beautiful sink to be empty and clean so we can feel the gushing of the warm, clean water. For some people, it has been such a long time that they forgot what their shiny sink looks like or how wonderful the beautiful, sparkling, clean, warm water feels! Some may doubt that the faucet is open, but very few *deny* that a faucet exists!

There are two reasons why we have a *spiritual vibrational energy* within us. Firstly, it is a gift of Oneness. The faucet, the sink, the drain, and the water all belong and function perfectly together. If the sink was to crack or the drain got plugged, Oneness would still exist because the open water faucet would still flow. The plugged drain is the *only* thing that disrupts the water's flow. This disruption of flow puts the sink out of order or alignment. So, the first reason that our *spiritual vibrational energy* exists is to help us *recognize* that we have a plugged drain and that we are out of order or alignment. It is our *spiritual vibrational energy* that helps us *feel* that there is more to our physical existence, or that something isn't quite right, or that it's time for a change.

Secondly, the Divine Source gave us this gift of *spiritual vibrational energy* for the purpose of communication. It is intended to strengthen our relationship with our Divine Source to receive guidance to make life's existence easier and to help us connect to Oneness. It is through this communication that we continually receive unfathomable wisdom to assist us while we learn life's lessons, and feel incredible love which will raise our vibrational level to assist raising that of Oneness. Simply stated, *spiritual vibrational energy* is a communication tool.

In other words, our drain was created and given to us free of any debris. Through personal choices, decisions, and circumstances we plug our drain; we disrupt our *spiritual vibrational energy*. This perfect gift was given to us without any flaws, perfectly clean, and wholly functioning. Our *spiritual vibrational energy* is a gift that will never get broken or be taken from us. We may misplace it at times, but it is never lost.

We may forget how to hear, but it is never disconnected.

Slowly, as your drain becomes unplugged or as the gift of your *spiritual vibrational energy* becomes strengthened, it will become obvious that it will never die. It will remain a reflection of your true essence even after your body transitions in death. Therefore, there are two parts to the creation of a human being. The first part is the energy from our Divine Source called our *spiritual vibrational energy*, and the second part is our physical form called our body.

As your spiritually conscious instructor and mentor, with the assistance of my Choir, I am going to show you *how* to unplug your drain! In other words, I am going to show you how to recognize and reconnect with your *spiritual vibrational energy*. You may be asking yourself, *where is my drain?* Your drain is attached to the sink. As you know, symbolically your drain is your *spiritual vibrational energy* and your sink is your body and life. To unplug your drain or reconnect your *spiritual vibrational energy*, you must go through the dirty water of the sink to reach the drain. Going through the sink is the only way; the sink is your body ... your *mind*, to be exact, and that is where we are going next!

CHAPTER FOUR

The Human Body

Our *spiritual vibrational energy* is a huge open line and direct connection between our Divine Source and a tool we call our body. Without the physical form of a body we cannot *act* upon the messages we hear, and therefore we *can't learn* what we were put here to do. We cannot live as we were designed to do. Our creation happened for one reason: to live in *spiritual consciousness.*

When a man and woman come together to reproduce, their union initiates the formation of a *spiritual vibrational energy* that is an extension of our Divine Source. The flesh of that child's body contains part of the man and part of the woman. As children grow into adulthood, their experiences may take them farther away from the Divine Source, slowly deteriorating that line that once was clear and open. Life becomes filled with traumas and unfulfilled, painful, searching journeys, and many dead ends. Whether your life's journey was filled with pain or very rewarding, after the body transitions to death, the *spiritual vibrational energy* does not die with the body. It still communicates effortlessly and can still be felt after the body is gone. This entire process is the miracle of life!

The body has one main purpose, and that is to cultivate relationships.

It is through relationships that our body learns valuable lessons which will either strengthen or diminish our *spiritual vibrational energy*. There are three functions for the physical body. First, to be used as a tool to cultivate relationships, learn life lessons, and reproduce. Second, to encapsulate your *spiritual vibrational energy*, allowing your body to use this tool to communicate with our Divine Source and strengthen a relationship with our Divine Source. Third, to act as a protective shell for your vital organs, ensuring physical survival and allowing you to participate as an individual within Oneness.

For whatever reason, if you are not using your body as described in the above functions, as it was intended to be used, then you are incorrectly utilizing your body. Therefore, most likely your life is out of alignment, you have difficulties, illness, or hardships—so please consider your drain plugged and your sink slightly cracked! Put another way, the huge open line of communication and a direct, strong, loving connection between the Divine Source and you is diminished and clouded, leaving your current life situation not as happy, healthy, or prosperous as you would like! Therefore, your *spiritual vibrational energy* is diminished and clouded and just needs a little polishing!

If we keep to the analogy and call your *spiritual vibrational energy* a plugged drain, then upon death, would you think that your plugged drain would become clear or would it remain filled with debris? As you might guess, it will be perfectly clear as it was originally given to you. *You* filled it up with the harsh, cruel, and sad situations of your own life experiences, but *you* will not be penalized for *not* cleaning it out. You will not have *any* memory of *any* of life's cruel circumstances.

So why do I want to reconnect my spiritual vibrational energy ... or clean out my drain? Reconnecting your *spiritual vibrational energy* is the body's tool for communicating with the Divine Source. In fluid communication you will receive unfathomable knowledge, life lessons will become easier, and upon the transition to death there will be no fear. The rest of your life will be much better.

How do I reconnect the line of communication between me and the Divine Source? Your reconnection will automatically come. It is a very simple process of *recognizing* a shift—a *spiritual vibrational shift*. You have numerous opportunities every day to recognize and practice feeling a *spiritual vibrational shift!*

Now we know we want to open the line of communication and strengthen the connection between the Divine Source and ourselves. Basically, we *know* we have a drain and that it is plugged. In order to clear that drain we must go through the dirty water of the sink to reach the drain. In other words, our *spiritual vibrational energy* is diminished due to our harsh life experiences. The cruelties of our life were experienced by our body and lodged in our mind. Our mind takes our emotions and spins them into perceptions. Change the perceptions, change the emotions; change the emotions, remove the debris!

Learning how to deal with the physical body is a critical part of learning how to live in *spiritual consciousness*. The *body* is a *tool* for *feeling energy*. One of the most important organs that our body needs to protect is our brain. It is the brain that holds our incredibly powerful mind. When our body transitions to death, *everything* contained in your mind transitions too. You will have no past memories, thoughts, or feelings perceived with your five senses, or any emotions connected to the five senses. The only thing that survives the transition of death is our *spiritual vibrational energy*.

Our *spiritual vibrational energy* is a gift directly from the Divine Source and isn't capable of errors, as it is an extension of Divine Oneness. However, the mind and the body are reproduced from man and capable of errors. The mind is based in the emotions of the five human senses and capable of *errors in perception*.

If we are going to hear Divine messages, then we need to learn *how* our mind translates *what* it hears to *what* it feels; we need to learn about the perceptions in the mind in order to minimize our errors when translating. It is in learning about the mind's perceptions and recognizing errors that a natural, powerful, automatic shift in thinking will occur. Once a vibrational shift occurs, *spiritual consciousness* is bestowed upon you.

Again, *spiritual consciousness* is a unique state of living. It allows you to be in the moment, fully aware, with your senses highly acute, and your intuition peaking. In this consciousness, you are able to experience incredible visions, divine wisdom, knowledge, and surreal peace. *Spiritual consciousness* is a human state of living and *being*. It does not exist in death and it exists only on this earthly plane.

The purpose of this book is to teach you how to recognize a *spiritual vibrational shift* and the goal of this book is to obtain *spiritual consciousness*. In order to do that, you need to understand where it all begins, and that is your mind. Once you understand your mind, the goal of attaining *spiritual consciousness* will be within your grasp!

Let me please remind you that growing spiritually is not the same as learning a math equation or learning another language. It takes time and patience. This is the part where you are now doing and thinking. Reading might take you a little longer but you will get there, I promise. Stick with me!

* * *

CHAPTER FIVE

The Mind

We are more than halfway through our journey, so let me quickly recap what we have covered so far. We were all equally created from a Divine Source. We are all part of Oneness. There are two parts to a human being: energy from a Divine Source called *spiritual vibrational energy* and a physical body procreated by man.

Our *spiritual vibrational energy* comes directly from a Divine Source, is an open line of communication, isn't capable of errors, and allows us to hear the wisdom to assist us in learning life's lessons. It isn't capable of transition; its felt long after the body dies, and needs the *mind* to hear the messages and the *body* to feel the energy. The purpose of its existence is divine communication.

The second part to a human being is our physical body that is reproduced by man and is needed as a protective shell for many important organs; the brain is the organ that holds the mind, which is capable of errors, and when *spiritual vibrational energy* is out of alignment with the Divine Source, our body and its life will be in disharmony, pain, illness, etc. The purpose of bodily existence is to cultivate relationships.

In order to open our *vibrational spiritual energy* to allow our body to feel the messages accurately, the mind needs a shift in thinking. This shift is a natural shift that takes place through a process of recognition. When the mind recognizes a Trauma with a Struggle and then Searches for relief, a natural thinking Shift will automatically occur. This is called a *spiritual vibrational shift*. Then Resolution and peace will follow! Remember: a spiritual vibrational shift is *{anything that causes or makes to cause a re-closeness, reuniting, reconnectivity back to the Divine Source from once you were}*.

The end result of a *spiritual vibrational shift* is the beginning of ultimate peace. Our desire to reopen the line of communication, strengthen our relationship with the Divine Source, and live in a heightened state of spiritual awareness is called *spiritual consciousness*. Living in *spiritual consciousness* involves our body feeling messages that our mind perceives. Therefore, *spiritual consciousness* is the feelings *of* the body, receiving messages *in* the mind, from higher *spiritual vibrational energies*.

We are capable of incorrectly translating any messages that we receive from the Divine Source through our *spiritual vibrational energy*. I began searching for a way to *accurately communicate* with such wisdom and I wanted to know what seemed to hinder me from achieving accurate communication.

Earlier, I gave you the analogy of an open faucet, water, sink, and drain. Similarly, let me share how *I* logically explain consciousness, spiritual consciousness, the brain, and the mind. Remember, this is only my personal perspective based on surviving an NDE.

Consciousness

In a very general sense, consciousness is a state of being, doing, acting, and feeling while having the knowledge to separate a thought from a perception and knowing that you are doing it in that moment.

Spiritual Consciousness

Spiritual consciousness is a unique mode of living that allows you to be in the moment, fully aware, with your senses highly acute, and your intuition peaking. In *spiritual consciousness* you are able to experience incredible visions, divine wisdom, knowledge, and surreal peace. *Spiritual consciousness* is a human state of living and *being*. It does not exist in death and it exists only on this earthly plane.

The Brain

The *brain* is different from the mind; they are two separate entities. The brain is the organ that holds the mind; the brain is not tainted by the mind. The brain doesn't seem to be accurate, is capable of incorrectly processing information, and appears to be flawed.

After my NDE, I realized that the brain is a flawed tool of the body and does not exist when you die. It is not capable of holding memory upon death. The brain doesn't hold emotion. If it did, the night I died I would have felt love for my husband and concern for my son. But none of these emotions were present. I reasoned that if the brain doesn't hold memory, logic, or emotion, then its sole purpose must be like that of a command center overseeing all the organs and systems in the body. So if *spiritual consciousness* was not within the organ called my brain, was it within my mind?

The Mind

If the mind holds intellect, memory, and thoughts, then when I died, why didn't I know my dad was dead? Why did I not have a *mindful thought* that *I* was dead? The answer to that is because your mind is part of the body, and when the body dies so does your mind.

So how did I have the ability to communicate without a mouth, or maintain an awareness of communication or feel any other emotion besides love and peace? If I had an imagination while dead, then I certainly wouldn't have chosen to see my dad. I would much rather have seen Elvis, Michael Jackson, or JFK!

The brain's purpose is to hold our mind and act as a command center for the other organs within our body. The mind's purpose is to process information we receive from the brain. The brain receives information without processing it for accuracy, and then sends it to the mind, which is intellect, thoughts, memories, emotions, fears, and imagination. The mind then takes this information and spins it into our perception or thought.

It is at this exact point that our fears, anxiety, anger, compassion, empathy, and our logic reside. It is here that we must explore our warped sense of perception, which is causing all our pain. It is here that our drain begins to plug!

The mind seems to have two states of being. In the first state, you can allow your mind to go on *auto pilot*, allowing you to perform mundane tasks without any effort in thinking. It is in this state that perceptions run wild and logic's gatekeeper is sleeping. This part of the mind is always yapping in a dysfunctional mode. Unfortunately, this is the state of mind that most of us are in throughout our waking hours. This state of mind I like to call **mindless consciousness**.

The second state of being is what I call **alert consciousness**. In this state, you can live fully in each moment, completely conscious of the information the brain receives and in total control, recognizing the mind's misleading perceptions while making gentle corrections. In *alert consciousness*, the mind acknowledges its flaws and accepts corrections. But then the yappy *mindless consciousness* takes over and shuts out *alert consciousness*, making it hard to hear messages or feel *spiritual consciousness*.

I knew that to accurately communicate with a higher vibrational level of wisdom, I needed to learn more about *alert consciousness* and *mindless consciousness*. When my mind was in *alert consciousness* I could clearly hear the wisdom, life was easy, and I had no fear or depression. Then—without my even realizing it—fear, anger, and pain were back and

I was in *mindless consciousness* again.

What was it going to take to keep me in *spiritual consciousness* at all times, not just in fleeting moments here and there? Then, I figured it out!

* * *

CHAPTER SIX

Spiritual Consciousness

*I*t was quite easy to find *spiritual consciousness*, but what became difficult was staying in it. It seemed one minute I was perfectly content without fear and depression. Then the next minute, I found myself back where I hated being. Why?

First of all, becoming *spiritually conscious* is a mentally conscious decision to develop and grow your own *spiritual vibrational energy*. It isn't thrust upon you, surprising you one day when you wake up. You will need to work at it, show it some effort, and be patient about growth. Not knowing any better, I put such unrealistic expectations upon my growth that the process became much harder and more painful than necessary. If you try to force spiritual growth, the process will take longer. Enjoy the journey.

Secondly, it is very important to understand the body is a vessel for communication. Not just the mind, but the whole body. That is why we need to take care of our vessel, our body. Eat right, exercise, drink plenty of fluids, no alcohol or drugs. Try to live as cleanly as possible. The clarity of what you will receive will be only as good as the vessel it is sent to.

Since my NDE, I don't eat much red meat. I have noticed a huge change in my clarity, my body, and my energy level. Although I do not eat red meat, and I am not a vegetarian, I would suggest limiting the quantity of red meat in your diet for a couple of weeks and see how *you* feel.

Thirdly, if you understand and are able to recognize that there are two states of being of the mind, *mindless consciousness* and *alert consciousness*, then you will enjoy many vibrational shifts. It is only in *alert consciousness* that your mind is capable of recognizing errors and celebrating vibrational shifts. The only thing that prevents you from any sort of success is your *mindless consciousness*. It is here where fear, anxiety, debt, and illness lie.

So what is the difference between *alert consciousness* and *spiritual consciousness*?

Alert consciousness is a tool of the mind that allows us to connect directly to our *spiritual vibrational energy* and the *spiritual vibrational energy* of others. Although it is capable of errors, it is also capable of correction and recognition of truth. It is like a muscle that needs to be worked every day; if it is not worked, the yappy *mindless consciousness* temporarily takes over. Everyone has been in *alert consciousness* at some point without even recognizing it. It is through *recognizing* that this state exists that we can remain in *alert consciousness*. Once in the state of *alert consciousness* you can hear/feel *spiritual consciousness*.

The main difference between the two is that *alert consciousness* is capable of recognizing errors and is the *only* place where corrections can be made. **Spiritual consciousness** understands unfathomable wisdom from our Divine Source wherein error doesn't exist. Unlike *alert consciousness*, which can be shut off by the yappy *mindless consciousness*, the information within *spiritual consciousness* is always flowing, waiting to be heard.

Spiritual consciousness is another tool of the mind that allows you to hear or feel the unfathomable messages from our Divine Source. As *alert consciousness* connects to *spiritual vibrational energy,* this tool called *spiritual consciousness* allows you to hear or feel messages that our Divine

Source or deceased loved ones want you to feel or hear.

Sometimes, without realizing it, when your mind is alert you will get messages or feel very profound thoughts that may catch you by surprise. The minute you stop and try to get them back again, they are gone. Why? It is because your mind has gone from being alert and in the moment to thinking and processing. It went from alert to mindless very quickly without recognizing the change.

What are the similarities between *alert* and *spiritual consciousness*?

Alert consciousness and *spiritual consciousness* are both of the mind, are unable to survive the transition of death, and are both created to enable direct communication with our Divine Source. Although each has a different function, they both have the same purpose: communication.

Since the purpose of *alert consciousness* and *spiritual consciousness* is communication, try to think of them as being like a telephone line and telephone receiver. *Alert consciousness* is the telephone receiver which allows you the ability to have a conversation with many. But in order to hear the conversation you need to hook that receiver up to a telephone line.

Spiritual consciousness is like your telephone line allowing you to enjoy a flowing conversation. If something were to happen to the telephone line, you would no longer hear the conversation. It doesn't mean that the conversation isn't there; it just means that you can't hear it.

The same is true for having a receiver but no telephone line. You may have a very strong desire to have a conversation, but if the line is down, communication is impossible. It is part of the miracle of life that we were *ALL* blessed with a telephone line and receiver; we just don't always know how to use them at the same time.

If you were to be shown once how to put them together then the rest would fall perfectly into place and you would never lose the communication again. Once you have it, you will never lose it. I promise.

* * *

Throughout most of my life, except for a few fleeting moments, most of my life was lived in *mindless consciousness*. Immediately following the trauma of my NDE, my perception was drastically altered by the experience and for some reason my mind was thrown into permanent *alert consciousness*.

However, in order to *fit in* again and go *back to normal*, my mind needed to switch back to *mindless consciousness*—and then the painful war began. When I tried to go back to my old routine and live in *mindless consciousness*, I found only anger, confusion, and serious depression, which again threw my perceptions into chaos.

As my research reassured me that what I was feeling was *normal*, I began to surrender and accept it. Although I understood and accepted my new state as *normal*, the after-effects of my NDE left me overwhelmed by trying to cope with life. My *mindless consciousness* screamed that I was *abnormal*, and my fear and insecurity seemed constant.

I realized that just accepting or surrendering to a situation, and having your pain validated, isn't enough. You must consciously recognize both states of consciousness and a shift *must* occur in your current state of thinking.

It is through *recognizing* alert consciousness that a thinking shift *will* take hold in your mind. The thinking shift is called a *spiritual vibrational shift*. Without recognizing this shift you cannot experience *spiritual consciousness*, heightened awareness, and a developed communication link between the Divine Source and yourself.

Becoming aware that you *are* aware, or *recognizing* that you have *recognized*, is all that you have to do. I will give you a step-by-step guide showing *how* I first started and *how* I *continue* to stay in a *state of recognizing*, or spiritual consciousness!

* * *

CHAPTER SEVEN

Spiritual Vibrational Shift

I believe we all struggle with change. We are creatures of habit. Without any warning, one of life's circumstances could thrust a change upon us, creating some sort of pain, disharmony, discomfort, or great joy that we aren't used to. You might have experienced a radical, unexpected change like getting news from your doctor about a terminal illness. Or a slow-brewing change might have just erupted into full crisis without warning. In any case, we seem to get caught off guard.

It is when we get caught off guard that we go into denial. It is denial that keeps us locked in pain and prolongs our healing. When I woke up the morning of my NDE, I did not know what might lie ahead of me and I certainly couldn't have predicted that SVT! However, immediately following my NDE I knew that my life was very different and my need for help was overwhelming. My denial kept me locked in depression. The moment I surrendered and accepted that my changes weren't going away, *this* process started. Recognizing and practicing *alert consciousness* began my healing.

Right now it doesn't matter what life circumstance has been thrust upon you; marriage difficulties, divorce, loss of purpose, winning the lottery, death of a loved one, retirement, searching for a soul mate, bankruptcy, new baby struggles, weight issues, being fired from a job, NDE, lack of self-confidence, or just being mad at God. The simple act of *seeking* will enable you to find *your* answers.

And so, my friends, because this book is in your hands, real change will happen, barriers can be removed, and blind faith can be given to *this* process. Allow this new information to resonate within you, be inspired by true change for your highest good. When you make a mental, conscious choice to understand these important concepts, and practice what you have learned, you *will* enjoy the state of *spiritual consciousness*. Try it, and you will see it for yourself!

The most important thing to know is that to obtain *any* shift in thinking you must first consciously recognize that you want and need a change. You must be passionate about creating a change and be brutally honest with yourself. If you aren't, you will be going through the motions and there will be nothing authentic about the change. Nor will it last.

The remainder of Part Two is going to teach you about *spiritual vibrational shifts*. A natural change in thinking is called a *shift*. Remember: what I call a **spiritual vibrational shift** is *{anything that causes or makes to cause a re-closeness, reuniting, reconnectivity back to the Divine Source from once you were}. Any* spiritual vibrational shift that causes you to experience spiritual intuitiveness, heightened energy levels, and psychic awareness puts you in a state of higher consciousness. Attaining *spiritual consciousness* is our goal.

You don't think that *you know* this stuff, which is why I am only *reminding* you. Because *I know* that you do *know* this stuff. I don't expect you to *know* what to do. I want you to *do nothing* but allow all that you read to be absorbed! A *spiritual vibrational shift* is taught through recognition.

Recognition is brought to us by using the tools of our mind. There are two tools of the mind that we *unknowingly* use on a daily basis, called our *alert consciousness* and *mindless consciousness*. Our *mindless consciousness* is going to *trigger* one or more of our emotions.

A *trigger* is like a warning signal; the louder the warning signals the more you need to be alert to the fact that an opportunity to recognize exists. The size of the *trigger* will depend on your own personal emotional reactions. Your emotional reaction is like a gauge of seriousness. The *trigger* consists of the conflict, disagreements, or traumas in your everyday life.

The *mindless consciousness* warns us with a trigger, and the *alert consciousness* eliminates the trigger.

That is why we need both facets of our mind. Don't worry if you don't remember definitions or all the labels. All of this information is just background; the remaining chapters will make perfect sense. You don't need to do anything; I will *show* you what both sides feel like! You just need to simply recognize when something makes you happy or sad. That's it! You can do this.

Many people live *only on* the side of *mindless consciousness*, so there is an abundance of triggers for you to choose from! An outline of the process is very simple and looks like this: Your life or body will experience an unwanted trauma (crisis). You will struggle with emotional triggers in life, such as fear or anger. You will search for a way to get rid of the emotionally painful triggers. Then, if a shift of some sort happens, like an apology, you will be happy again and have resolution—until the next trigger! If no shift of any kind takes place then you will be emotionally stuck!

As I described earlier, my NDE was my *Trauma*, the *Struggle* was my after-effects, and my *Search* was to eliminate my fear. My motivation was to abolish the pain, anger, frustration, loneliness, isolation, depression, bitterness, and guilt. The *spiritual vibrational shift* came when I recognized that I needed to recognize, and then I was able to surrender to my *new normal*. Now I am in *Peace* and *Resolution*. I celebrate living in *spiritual consciousness!* It's not our painful or traumatic individual experiences that matter, it's the *motivation* that fuels your *search*, and it's a *conscious decision* to *choose* to *recognize* a *spiritual vibrational shift.*

The goal of this book is to help you to attain *spiritual consciousness.* The purpose is to *remind* you that you already know what a *spiritual vibrational shift* is. You will see that I am not showing you anything new. But I am going to teach you the one small step that we all miss, and that is to *recognize* that you are recognizing! That too is very easy; come along and see for yourself! This is what sets this book apart from all the others.

To move on, let's assume that you *are* passionately motivated, you *are* on a search for answers, and you have *chosen* that you *want* to learn *how* to recognize that one small step. The only prerequisite is that you need to be able to recognize your emotion. You need to know that if something good happens, you *know* you feel happy, if something sad happens, you *know* you are sad. That's it! Then you are ready!

As you spiritually continue to grow, long after you close this book, it is my hope that you will always remember that you *never* quit spiritually growing. You will always remain an incredible creation, an extension of our Divine Source, and that you are filled with unfathomable wisdom, love, and patience. You and I are connected through Oneness. There is nothing you have to *learn*; you must *merely* remember. You will *not* be alone: as *you* journey through this process, the Divine Source, Oneness, and I will be cheering you on all the way ... forever! There are no right or wrong ways, only the way that is perfect for you.

* * *

CHAPTER EIGHT

Something to Recognize

*R*ecognizing a *very small step* is so simple, but it is incredibly easy to overlook and even harder to describe. The fact that it is capable of being overlooked doesn't mean that it doesn't exist. It always has existed; and it always will exist!

My definition of *recognizing* is: *consciously knowing* something, **and then** *consciously acknowledging that which you recognized.* I know it sounds like a brain twister, but stay with me. I am going to show you what I mean through examples and repetition.

Let's break down my definition. The first part: *consciously knowing something.* This is your perception of a thought, emotion, idea, or fear that was registered in your mind. It is either registered in the *mindless side* or the *alert side* of your consciousness. *And* you *know* that this thought, emotion, idea, or fear is there. This is the first part to finding that little step.

The second part of my definition: **and then** *consciously acknowledging that which you recognized.* The *consciously acknowledging that IS* the small little step.... This *is* recognizing!

Once you can understand this and actually do it *just once* ... you will *feel* a *spiritual vibrational shift*. Depending how blocked your line of communication is, you will feel it *immediately*. Continue doing it, and before long, your drain will no longer be blocked, you will enjoy a clean, open, bright, free-flowing direct connection to the Divine Source and other higher spiritual vibrational beings. Your questions will be answered, your fear eliminated, your relationships restored, and you will have an urge to share what you know. That is our purpose in Oneness! I did not create this ... I just remembered it so I could share it with you!

Why is this so hard? Don't worry. I am going to teach you! There is nothing that can't be understood with a little bit of patience and practice. I am going to show you *how* to make this easy on a daily basis, so you never forget again! This chapter will give you some examples that might prompt a search and show you how to assess whether your current situation is screaming for relief. In Oneness, we are all searching at one point or another. First, you need *something* to recognize. If your life were perfect, you would have nothing to recognize or learn. Second, recognize when your situation is screaming at you, in order to know when it is time to seek relief.

Any time our perception of our identity gets challenged or destroyed by some sort of situation, a disruption in our comfortable daily routine can cause us to feel despair, stress, anxiety, worry, helplessness, and maybe even fear. This may be enough to prompt a search for relief. A trauma does not have to be extreme. For example, it could be as simple as retiring from a job or winning the lottery. The first few months might be wonderful, but as time passes it will feel that there is no longer a purpose or a reason for getting up each morning. This interruption in lifestyle and routine can cause grief and bewilderment. Consciously or unconsciously, a search begins to find a new routine.

An exciting change could be a career woman deciding to start her family. She is looking forward to staying home to raise her children. Although the change was planned and anticipated, there is a huge disturbance in her new role or identity, and the loss of the freedom she once took for granted can be overwhelming. Again, the change from her old paradigm can leave her searching for her new identity.

It is the same for parents when their children finally leave home; this can be a hard transition. The shift from having children at home to an empty house can be very difficult and may leave the parent(s) pondering their new purpose in life. But the trauma I most often hear about is the death of an important loved one. If the deceased was hugely significant and was relied upon for love, sharing, emotional and financial support, this loss is devastating! Even with the passage of time, for some it will take years to overcome, while others will grieve their loss for the remainder of their lives.

When our situation or comfort zone is challenged, we will feel our emotions screaming at us to make a change. If you choose not to recognize it, to deny it, or avoid it, not only will your emotions be screaming at you, other areas of your life will begin to crumble. It is while you are assessing whether your situation is screaming at you, and you feel as if you are gasping for oxygen, that you need a shift in thinking.

Gasping for a shift in thinking is not unlike gasping for oxygen. We are surrounded by oxygen all day long. You can't see it but you know that it is there because you *can* breathe. If for some reason, the oxygen levels drop, you will know that something is terribly wrong. You will begin to gasp for air, and you will continue to gasp for air until you figure it out. Needing to *recognize* is like needing oxygen. Oxygen and recognition both fully surround us at all times, and if either is removed, we will begin to gasp. You get warning signals of the *need to recognize* throughout the day, without even knowing it.

As with our air, when there is not enough recognition, we begin to gasp. We might do things like take in a couple of deep breaths, take a quick pee break, sneak away for a cigarette, or stand up and stretch. Something is telling us *it's time for a break*, much as if we were gasping for air. When we finally do succumb and take in a breath or a quick pee break then we feel instant relief. It is through this *recognition* that we find relief.

Now we are going to use the example above to illustrate how we can recognize that small little step. Example: I *know* I was gasping for breath, I *know* I needed relief, and I *know* air was my relief.

Now for that little step: ....right now in this moment.... I know I got air.....I know....that I know.....that I got air.

The second step is the *need* to *consciously acknowledge* that which you *just recognized.* I don't want you to recognize *what happened* but that you know ... it happened.

There is *a moment in time* when you are actively, consciously acknowledging all that you recognize. It is that *moment*, that brief second, in which this second step takes place. It is so easy to miss. You only have to be introduced to it once to always have it. Once you find it, it will never leave you! Spiritual growth is slow, needs time, and requires patience. It will not be rushed; you are doing great, hang in there!

I am going to show you how I found my *moment in time*. Once I found the *moment in time*, the second step hit me right in the head. So the next part of your journey is showing you where I found my *moment in time* and how you can find yours!

* * *

CHAPTER NINE

Triggers

We don't feel peace on a consistent basis because, for the most part, we exist in *mindless consciousness*. We are too busy raising children, cooking dinner, working long hours to pay the bills, arguing, meeting deadlines, cleaning the house, working two jobs, and caring for other people. We can't feel a *moment in time* because we are not in the right frame of mind. We need to re-train our brains to perceive situations differently, learn to recognize warning signals, and make an effort to find a quiet moment within every hectic day. This chapter is about learning how to find and stay in *a moment in time* or *alert consciousness*.

I believe there are three main reasons why we don't try to find *a moment in time*. We don't know how to. We don't know why we should. Or we just don't care to.

If you don't know *why* you should or don't know *how* to find a *moment in time*, don't worry. Through our journey together, you will find out how I found it and why it is so important. If you just don't care to … then anything that I tell you from this point on will probably sound like mumbo jumbo!

Why is a *Moment in Time* Important?

The purpose of silence is to find a quiet *moment in time*. The purpose of finding a *moment in time* is to find the clarity of *spiritual consciousness*. The most important reason why we need to find a *moment in time* is for the well-being of our relationships. Without the clarity of a moment in time, *all* relationships suffer. They suffer because without the moment of clarity there would be no apologies, unconditional love, or forgiveness. Oneness would become a weakened state of the whole.

I am sure we can all agree that life is too hectic at times. We *know* what the problem is. We just don't know *how to slow it down*. Now more than ever, it is critically important to find some silence. Find some opportunities for free, quiet time. We all need to regroup, ground ourselves, take a time out, find a fresh start, and try to rejuvenate our batteries.

If you do choose to make even small opportunities for free quiet time, you will feel less stressed; you will be happier, will make decisions easier, will parent your children better, and find patience such as you have never known.

The time I speak of is not hours every day. It is only a few quick minutes; it is not the length of time or place that this moment is taken that is important. The most important aspects are that you are consciously deciding to take a break and what you *do* with this break.

How Do I Find a *Moment in Time*?
Recognizing the Warning Signals

Personally, I love the word *trigger*, and my perception of that word reminds me of my SVT warning signals. As you could imagine, I had numerous warning signals that I ignored, probably because I refused to *make* the *time* to stop and listen.

We must first recognize some of *our personal* warning signals, which hereafter we will call *triggers*. A *trigger* will feel like stress, anger, hostility, pain, grief, rage, frustration, over-excitability, or the worst one, fear. A *trigger* will start off so quietly that you may not even notice, but it will continue to get louder and louder until it escalates into full-blown anger, sadness, hostility, or fear. The trick is to recognize the *trigger* before it climaxes.

Recognize when someone or something makes you angry, or if something you see or read *triggers* sadness, or if an interaction with a perfect stranger leaves you frustrated. Recognize **only how you are feeling.** Many times we try to psychoanalyze the other person or the situation because we don't want to face the accountability for how **we** are feeling. It is accepting accountability for our feelings that forces us to feel responsible for doing something. And often we resist what we *perceive to be* the forced responsibility of *doing* what we don't want to do... so we deny the feeling.

Please just be mindful that your *button has been pushed*, and no matter what the situation or person, something has *triggered* an unwanted emotion. Unfortunately, being human, we tend to overlook these warning signals. All that I am suggesting is that you recognize *how* you are feeling. Is the situation or person making you feel mad, frustrated, happy, peaceful, hostile, or furious?

For the time being, right now, the *why or the reason* doesn't matter. The only thing that matters is that you are recognizing this *trigger* and validating your feelings. We will get into what to do with those feelings later on, but for now, just be mindful of when you feel like you are gasping for air or *need to take a minute*.

Recognize That you are Taking a *Moment in Time*

You recognize that you are taking a moment in time when someone or some situation has *triggered* you and you need a quick second to acknowledge it. You are recognizing, in that split second, that this person or this situation is really frustrating or maddening. Some people may say *give me a minute* or *I just need a second*. It doesn't matter how we label it or what we call it. The most important thing is that when you recognized that you were negatively *triggered* by someone or something, you took a quick, brief, quiet moment to acknowledge it. That is it. It's that simple, I promise!

It is the act of *recognizing* that truly matters—don't suppress it. It is all right that it is there. This is not a lengthy process that takes hours; it is done in the blink of an eye. So now you recognize that this person or situation is drawing an unwanted emotion from you, and in recognizing this you've taken a brief moment. What do you **do** in this moment?

So far we've learned that our life is too hectic and we need to take a few brief, guilt-free moments out of our schedule. We can recognize triggers that act as warning signals. A situation or person either positively or negatively stimulates our emotions, and this is known as being triggered. Once you are triggered, you knowingly take a quick second to consciously recognize that you were triggered. Great job so far: so now what should you do in that moment in time? You are angry, frustrated, sad....

* * *

CHAPTER TEN

In the
Moment

Depending on your home life, if you have children or grandchildren, whether you own a home or rent, live independently or in shared accommodation, you *will* come into contact with other people. If you work one job or two, or if you are now retired, you will have contact with other human beings. Even if you are a recluse, you still need groceries, you still need to pay your bills, answer the door for the postman or watch television. You too will have contact with people, in one way or another.

Based on the law of probability, at some point in your life, you would have been *triggered*. Depending on your occupation or lifestyle, some of us have been *triggered* a lot more than others. A trigger is your emotional gauge, acting like a warning signal of anger, frustration, happiness, fear, or vengefulness.

Let me share with you an example of my recognizing my trigger and choosing what to do in the moment. It was *after* my NDE *and* living in *spiritual consciousness.* It was mid-afternoon on Easter weekend, and I needed a few groceries. The store was packed with people, many rushing around for their last-minute dinner preparations. The checkout lineups were very long, the cashiers looked tired, and the shoppers were frustrated.

As I stood in line with my few items, the shopper in front of me had a small child in the front of her cart and the back packed full with groceries. I noticed she placed each item slowly on the conveyer, one at a time. I was very conscious of how I was feeling but couldn't stop myself from naturally wondering why she was going so slowly. Her little boy, about three years old, was fussing, squirming, and whining to the point where I wanted to leave my groceries and just go.

After approximately ten minutes, my patience was drawing to a close, my frustration level was peaking, and my anger was starting to boil. I felt she was very disrespectful of everyone in our line as she took her sweet time to unload her huge shopping cart. I felt angry that she had no regard for her poor small son, who was now reeling with his own frustration.

After her cart was almost empty, I realized that my warning bells were screaming at me—I was *triggered*. Recognizing this, I tipped my head all the way back, looked up to the ceiling (a bit reminiscent of where Heaven is!), took a deep breath, and as I exhaled on my second deep breath I brought my head back into the situation.

I was in a different perspective. *Only now,* in this perspective, did I realize that she was adding up the cost of her groceries as she was putting them on the conveyer to ensure she had enough money. My thoughts were no longer of anger, frustration, or lack of respect but rather the opposite. I found myself very proud of her for taking such financial responsibility. I felt very humbled and grateful that I didn't have to count each penny that I spent, and I felt guilty that I'd had ill feelings toward her.

So in my moment, I chose to feel gratitude about where I was that day and how wonderful it was to learn from yet another *trigger*. How truly blessed I was that this stranger I had never seen before had taught me a lesson. I said a little prayer hoping that should I be faced with this type of situation again I would not be as judgmental. In my prayer, I asked our Divine Source to give this woman a wonderful Easter, health to her and all those she loves, happiness such as she has never felt before, and wealth—so she doesn't hold up another line!

Therefore, in the moment, you get to choose how you spend it. You will not be able to control where or when this moment takes place, and it doesn't matter where or when it happens. The only thing that matters is *WHAT* you do with this moment. Make the most of this time; have thoughts of gratitude, say a little prayer, think positive thoughts, find anything positive, or empathize with another ... or do all of the above!

We all must try to remember that we are all spiritual beings having a human experience. We were created equally and we exist together in Oneness. I personally look toward gratitude first. I try to find anything that I can be grateful for. Then I empathize with the person or situation. I find something positive—anything positive—then I say a little prayer. My prayer begins with what I've learned and a blessing to help me continue to learn, and then I send a blessing to that person or situation that I perceived to be causing my pain.

This is a good example for understanding *recognizing*. For right now, this very moment, the most important thing is that you recognized that someone or something *triggered* you negatively, and you took a quick, brief, quiet moment to acknowledge it, *and then* recognized that you'd recognized!

Remember that with each *trigger* you get to experience, each time you acknowledge a moment, you are that much closer to unblocking your drain. Triggers are debris stuck in your drain. Each trigger you acknowledge gives you more and more moments of clarity ... *spiritual consciousness*. So the next time something or someone *triggers* you, make a mental note that you are one step closer to feeling that sparkling, clean, warm water and a shiny, bright sink!

Important Exercise Before Moving On

During the next few days be mindful of when you are feeling *triggered*. The warning signals are stress, anger, hostility, pain, grief, rage, frustration, over-excitability, or fear. We are given numerous *triggers* before a situation escalates. Being human, we unfortunately overlook these *triggers*. For now, just be mindful of when you feel like you are gasping for air or need to take a minute, **and then** recognize that you are aware that you've been triggered.

* * *

CHAPTER ELEVEN

Recognizing All Triggers

The reason we start out by recognizing negative emotions is that they are the easiest to see right away. Negative emotions feed our yappy *mindless consciousness*. Basically, in order to starve the yappy side of our mind we need to understand when we are feeding it.

It is very exciting when you first begin to recognize the yappy side of your mind. So why do we have a yappy side if it causes us so much trouble? I am so grateful we all have a yappy *mindless consciousness* because without knowing the yappy side of our mind, how could we compare it to the loving, intuitive side of *alert consciousness*? It is only in understanding and learning about the yappy side that the other side makes its presence known.

As *alert consciousness* develops and time progresses, not only will you recognize *triggers,* but you will also recognize happiness, joy, innocence, bliss, gratitude, and contentment. More and more triggers will start to disappear, and soon you will only see innocence, bliss, gratitude, and contentment. You will be living more in *alert consciousness*.

Occasionally the yappy side will scream, but you will lovingly acknowledge it and put it away. You will automatically feel gratitude that the yappy side exists. The yappy *mindless consciousness* is a constant reminder to stay in *alert consciousness*, where peace, happiness, and infinite wisdom are in abundance.

We are going to deal with everyday situations that many of us are easily hurt by. This is also a wonderful opportunity to learn and recognize where painful trigger situations come from. You will learn through *my honesty* and *my painful triggers*. The more triggers we feel and acknowledge, the less we become triggered. The less we are triggered, the closer we are to *spiritual consciousness*. This is a chapter about recognizing and practicing if you **choose** to. It is here we see that the *proof is in the pudding*, so you can try it for yourself; put what I am saying to the test.

Let's start with a quick recap to see how far we have come. Our *spiritual vibrational energy* needs a shell to cover and protect it, and this is our body. Our body is the only thing capable of dying. One of the tools of our body is our brain, and within our brain is our mind. Within our mind is our consciousness. Our consciousness has two parts, and only *one* part can be activated and working at a time. The two parts to our consciousness are called *mindless consciousness* and *alert consciousness*.

The majority of people exist today within yappy *mindless consciousness*. In *mindless consciousness* you experience fear, anger, frustration, sadness, hopelessness, and confusion. The only way to let go of this yappy side of consciousness is through awareness and conscious change. *Mindless consciousness* prohibits us from having authentic, loving relationships with the Divine Source, others, and ourselves.

The second part to our consciousness is *alert consciousness*. It is here that we live in each moment with no regrets or guilt and are able to cherish all *beings*. It is here that *Oneness* is honoured and celebrated. *Alert consciousness* gives us the ability to obtain unfathomable wisdom and feel true love and peace, which is the same unconditional love and peace I felt during my NDE. In *alert consciousness* we can recognize the mistakes of the yappy side of our mind and make gentle corrections so we can flourish in love, health, and finances.

Developing the state of *alert consciousness* allows us to receive unfathomable wisdom rooted within our *spiritual vibrational energy*, which is a direct connection to our *Divine Source*. Once the developed state of *alert consciousness* exists, the ability to hear and feel messages of unfathomable love, wisdom, and peace from our Divine Source is called *spiritual consciousness*.

Now let's continue learning more about triggers. Becoming aware of *triggers* will develop and mature your *alert consciousness*. The purpose of this chapter is to expose what *triggers* are and begin the growth and development of *alert consciousness*.

It's not difficult to know that someone has *triggered* something inside of you. As soon as we are *triggered* we are quick to feel hurt, anger, fear, sadness, etc. Our physical purpose here on earth is to cultivate relationships—with our Divine Source, each of his creations, and ourselves.

The first and most important relationship is with our Divine Source. If we cannot hear or feel the messages of higher vibrational energies then we will not be as effective when dealing with others. The second most important relationship is with ourselves. Believe it or not, this can be the hardest, most unforgiving, self-sabotaging, negative, and unloving relationship we have today. Lastly, the third most important relationship is with Oneness. If you raise your *spiritual vibrational energy* level you will be raising that of mankind.

Relationships can be difficult, but once mastered they represent the true meaning to our physical existence and life on earth. I have broken down some common situations where *triggers* could occur and some potential reactions when they happen. We will learn about the negative emotions first because they are the easiest to illustrate.

I included the next couple of chapters because they represent some of the hardest lessons I've learned. Before my NDE, my views on these topics all resided in my yappy mind. I had no idea two sides even existed! After my experience, my reactions and *triggers* in these same scenarios changed dramatically, throwing my life into utter chaos.

It was around each of these topics that I experienced most of my triggers and pain. Since I am human like you, I suspect you will be able to empathize with me, and I hope you will appreciate my hardcore honesty. These chapters are important because it is in learning from my display of these painful triggers that you will become acutely aware of your own triggers.

* * *

CHAPTER TWELVE

Lack of Self-Worth and Validation

*I*t was eight months *after* my dad died and almost two years *before* my NDE that I began writing a journal. While watching an Oprah episode I realized that most of the famous guests she interviewed all wrote journals and seemed to "have it together."

With my husband constantly encouraging me, I began a journal, hoping to have it all come together for me too. My first journal entry was on December 19, 2008. I had just sold my real estate brokerage and wasn't able to transfer my licence to another brokerage until all the paperwork was submitted and approved by the government. This meant that I didn't have a job for a couple of weeks. It didn't matter to me; I was grateful and looking forward to a break and having it all come together ... but, as you will read, I was far from getting it together!

Journal entry: December 19, 2008:

What do I want? Good question. I believe that everything happens for a reason even though we may not know the reason. I am looking forward to these next few weeks off and to prepare for Christmas. My first Christmas without

Dad, how am I possibly going to do it? I know that life goes on and it has been a "reasonable" amount of time so I need to buck up and just get through it.

I miss my dad terribly, I feel so lost, my focus is drifting and I don't know what to do. There are no expectations of me any longer. I wish my dad were here, he'd tell me what I should be doing with my life. I have always focused on showing my dad that I was successful, I was smart, great in business, great mother, great wife, and great daughter and now I am a failure at them all. Dad, I have always done as you have asked even if it meant hardship to me or my family; now where the hell are you?

It's funny now that you're dead and I have just realized that no matter what I have ever done for you or shared with you, it was probably never good enough. You have always hated that we never went to church and you always seemed disappointed that I never made enough money, had a nice-enough home, had nice enough furniture, or saved enough money. Then there were other times you scolded me for being foolish with my money ... well now I have none either way, no matter what I achieved or what I didn't accomplish, it was never good enough. So now what? ...

My family looks to me to hold it all together, put on a happy face and make Christmas normal. How the hell am I going to keep it together? I don't have two nickels to rub together and even if I did, I still don't want to put up a tree or even cook stupid Christmas dinner. Christmas is a time for family but my dad is dead and no one seems to give a sh*t. Everyone is pretending that everything is normal and life *goes on. Well they can all kiss my a**. I'm not putting up a tree, cooking Christmas dinner or buying any presents, how is that for normal!? What the hell is wrong with me? Has my purpose in life been to show my dad that I am a good person? Have I always sought his approval? Now what am I supposed to do? I don't even know who I am anymore. Did I ever know who I am? How the hell did I get in this Godforsaken place?*

* * *

It wasn't until after my near-death experience that I re-read some of my journal entries, which I rarely share as they are very painful for me to read. It saddens me to think that my self-esteem, self-confidence, and sense of self-worth were all in the tank! However, I believe this is very normal for the majority of people. Self-worth is probably the biggest element that humans lack. We then compound our problem by seeking validation that we are worthy of love, kindness, compassion, empathy, and joy. When we don't receive any validation, we lose our sense of identity and we get easily triggered.

Everyone seeks validation in one way or another. Pay close attention to what others are saying. It might sound like: "I want to put my nice dress on because I don't want them to think I am a slob." Or: "Don't eat with your fingers; people will think you are a pig"; or "Comb your hair; we don't want people to think you just rolled out of bed"; or "If I share the after-effects of my NDE, people will think I am crazy!"

Now, since living in *spiritual consciousness*, do you know what I say to all of this? *WHO CARES*!? You know you're not a pig, or lazy, or a slob, and even if you are, then you should embrace it! If you don't like *who* you are then change it!

The lack of a positive self-image can be due to negative self-talk, manipulation within important relationships in our lives, or abuse by important people in our lives. Some other causes might be sexual abuse, bullying, lack of independence, disability, or an identity crisis. Regardless, the responsibility is yours to find out *who you are*. It is up to you to love yourself first, no matter what anyone else thinks, says, or does. This is the hard part, but it is done. If I can do it, so can you; stick with me!

Depending on the reason for your lack of self-image, watch for the trigger when strangers try to tell you *what to do* or *how to do it*. Pay attention to how you feel when you come in contact with someone you perceive as better than you, or who perceives that *they* are better than you. The trigger might involve you feeling defensive and guarded, being quick to judge, or because of your vulnerability, even trying to bully back. Recognizing triggers is the first step to finding yourself, finding *alert consciousness*.

These were some of my most painful areas that I felt were important to cover. Of course there are many more, but for now this will be our start.

* * *

CHAPTER THIRTEEN

Judging with Justification

*L*et's be perfectly clear. Being judgmental, even with justification, arises from the yappy side of consciousness and is purely unjustifiable under any circumstances. Being judgmental is rampant within our society, and it starts long before school begins. Kids can be cruel little creatures. Without comprehension, children learn this cruelty from the role models in their lives. Children who come from affluent backgrounds or poverty-stricken households learn very early who *their kind* is and who is not. It is here that the classes seem to divide. Little children today are our adults of tomorrow. This behaviour was learned without comprehension, and now it is time to reverse the innocent errors of our ways.

Let me explain. One day before my near-death experience, I was showing my client some houses. She was an older woman. We needed to pass through a rough part of town to get to our destination. As we drove by some homeless people and prostitutes, my client remarked, "Look at those people, I bet their mothers must be horrified ... I bet they don't even have mothers!" At the time, I agreed with her, thinking I was empathizing with those poor people down on their luck. I continued thinking that I was so grateful that I was not like *one of them*.

Another example is the abuse waitresses sometimes have to put up with from restaurant patrons. Some people think that a waitress/waiter is subservient to them because they are serving the meal. It may be their job to serve the meal, but it is certainly not their life's purpose!

Although uncomfortable to watch, it is a great learning lesson. Unless it is brought to our attention, most of us do not look for abusive patrons, nor do we want to see them. So the next time you go into any restaurant, try it, look for it, and it will probably trigger you. But don't let that lesson go to waste, learn from it. Remember, when we go to a restaurant we are paying for the food that the chef cooks; the service is just a bonus. The next time you see a homeless person or prostitute; do not take pity on them. They don't deserve your pity because they are no different than you and are a part of the same Oneness that you belong to.

Now, since my NDE and being spiritually conscious, I am amazed at my different thought processes and shocked at how I used to think. I no longer use words like *those people* or *like one of them* because we are all One. We all come from the same Divine Source, and we all contain a *spiritual vibrational energy*. Although our sleeping arrangements, occupations, and lifestyles may be different, we are all a part of Oneness— equally, no better or worse.

Think about it: When we feel pity for someone we are elevating ourselves above them. We are defining our life, living environment, and circumstances as better than theirs. In doing so, we automatically, without thinking, consider ourselves superior to them. And we certainly are not. If we can learn to separate the person from their lifestyle or circumstance, we can understand triggers a lot more easily.

A trigger involving judgment occurs when someone, without thinking, automatically elevates himself above you in any way. You feel lesser than, not as good as, or inferior to; this feeling creates a trigger … and a big one! Conversely, without even knowing it, you may elevate yourself above someone else. In doing so, you may initiate the same trigger in that other person. Recognizing judgment takes practice, so when you see it and recognize it know that you are that much closer to an authentic relationship with the Divine Source, with yourself, and with Oneness.

* * *

CHAPTER FOURTEEN

Guilt and Fear

uilt and fear are two horrible emotions that arise from the yappy *mindless consciousness*. It's primarily these two emotions that keep us from growing and feeling our *spiritual vibrational energy* and living in *alert consciousness*.

Guilt is debilitating. I shared with you, in Part One, my guilt about not spending more time with my grandmother. Her death had robbed me of ever making this up to her. Where did this guilt come from? Guilt is not only associated with death, but synonymous with relationships. It seems that where there is a relationship there is the potential for guilt; the stronger the relationship the deeper the guilt. Guilt is always present and wreaking havoc.

Parenting is also a potential source of guilt. *We did too much; we didn't do enough; I wasn't home enough*—where does it all end? The only good thing that can come from guilt is recognizing it and not allowing it to fester. Guilt can prevent us from living in the moment and cherishing everything in that moment.

The trigger of guilt could be blame, defensiveness, or shock, but most often it is anger. When someone we are in a relationship with tells us how they are feeling when *we* have wronged them, we might automatically, deep down, feel guilty. But our first reaction might be shock that it's even being discussed. From there we might become a little defensive; some might try to push the blame elsewhere or try to justify their actions. Others might jump straight to anger, or worse, avoidance. Either way, our deep-seated guilt, whether unfounded or not, needs to be acknowledged and accepted; and, a conscious decision to change it needs to occur before it can go away.

Fear is totally different but is just as debilitating. Some fears are definitely founded on good reason. Fear can be a good thing, a signal warning us to pay attention. It can also be unfounded and not based in reality. Fear is usually *time* based. We fear that we can't pay rent next month, or that something might happen to my son someday, or "How am I going to keep it all together when my dad dies?" Fear is of the past or the future. Fear is never *in the moment*; unless it is to act as an immediate warning signal of something that has yet to come.

It's true that our future is unknown and that life is unpredictable. This can cause fear, as it did for me. There are so many reasons why we may be fearful, and the vast extent of triggers associated with fear is a book in itself! The best generality I have come to realize about fear is that most of the time it is unfounded and created within the yappy, dysfunctional side of our mind.

A general trigger of fear arises when *your perception* of security gets challenged. Some challenges we may face is if the paycheck isn't enough to cover the bills, if the children get sick, if your spouse is cheating, if you were mocked and laughed at, if your home is in jeopardy, if you were unexpectedly disabled in some way, or if death or the threat of death is upon you. Your reaction to the trigger could be worry, anger, sadness, withdrawing from the world, and/or denial. Fear is probably going to be one of the first triggers you will recognize because it is the most prevalent within our world.

Here is an example of recognizing fear in the moment: The night I died, I was gripped with fear. I knew I was going to die but I couldn't seem to get my urgent message across. I was paralyzed with fear about what was going to happen ... in that moment. Was my fear founded? Maybe yes and maybe no; but for me at that moment in time it was founded; it was real, and it was going to happen sometime very soon.

So was I triggered? You bet I was! I was crying, angry, frustrated, short-tempered, and self-centered, because in that moment, I was the only thing that mattered in this world. I was overwhelmed with fear. Fear is real, and it can be debilitating and it needs to be addressed and conquered.

Here's an example of recognizing past or future fear: After my NDE, I did not like being around people at all. I had so much trouble going into public and feeling everyone's hostile energy. I was told that my NDE was a blessing, a gift from God, and a beautiful experience to treasure and learn from. In denying my experience, I denied the gift that it truly was. I had serious trouble coping with the psychological and physiological after-effects, which I actively denied existed, sometimes to the extent of even denying that my NDE had actually happened!

Other than the odd grocery shopping trip, I didn't leave the house for almost nine months! During that time I was so fearful that I would never fit in again; I constantly worried about the future. How am I going to work? How will I pay the bills? How do I go back to finding the old *Lorri*? We can see that it is easy to worry about the future—not justifiable, but very easy. The fear trigger is time-based and arises when your perception of security is challenged.

* * *

CHAPTER FIFTEEN

Grudges

A grudge is a feeling, one with propelling *action*. A grudge itself has the quality of action only in the sense of holding on, not letting go. In order for a grudge to be kept alive, we make a conscious decision to keep it alive, and then we actively work at it. A grudge is what our *yappy mindless consciousness* has created. It is the act of not forgetting, the activity of consciously keeping it. Grudges are alive only in the yappy side of your mind because there is no such thing as grudges in *alert consciousness*. Why? *Alert consciousness* does not deal with the past or think of the future but dwells only in forgiveness.

Let me share what I mean. Before my near-death experience I owned a real estate brokerage while my dad was actively dying. I was being pulled in so many directions: being a mom and wife, keeping a home, cooking dinner, washing clothes, paying the bills, and balancing the books. I was also a real estate agent, actively selling homes to my clients and listing homes for sale. I was also the broker and boss of the office, where I had to help my agents be successful with their careers and prepare and reconcile the office's trust accounts. I devoted half of my time to family, home, and work, and the other half to my dad. This went on for almost two years.

As my dad's condition worsened he was moved to hospice. I was obsessed with thoughts of losing him. I neglected all my daily responsibilities and put them on hold while I spent almost every waking hour with my dad for the last nine months of his life. My relationships suffered, my work suffered, my brokerage suffered. My dad was worried because I was spending so much time with him, and he wondered who was looking after the business. I assured Dad that I had made special arrangements with my business partner to stay at the brokerage and run it while I was away.

My business partner came to visit my dad at the hospital and in hospice a couple of times, and he reassured my dad that everything was fine and that the office was doing great. My dad and my business partner had a relationship that I envied. They spoke to each other as equals, with mutual respect and admiration. My dad was reassured that no matter what happened after he was gone, my business partner would be there for me. Although I was in horrible pain losing my dad, I was at least anchored at work.

After my dad passed away, I immediately returned to work. The brokerage was in serious financial ruin. My business partner had quit and left me to clean up the mess. When he left the company, he owed me money which he continually refused to pay. In not paying his debt, he forced me to take on a huge financial responsibility, which left me and my family almost destitute.

I was furious and resentful, and I hated what he'd done. I felt so betrayed. It was very difficult to separate the man from his actions. In hating what he did, I also found myself hating him every minute of every day. Any thought of him filled me with unspeakable rage. Every day I was dead broke, pushing off creditors, trying to sell the business, and working long hours with very little sleep, all the while still having SVTs. Every day was a reminder of how much I was in financial ruin, exhausted, and getting sicker because of my SVTs. Every day I hated this man for turning his back on me when I needed him most and lying to my dad while he was dying. To make matters even worse, my dad was dead and I missed him terribly.

This is hate; this is a grudge. I had a very powerful negative feeling toward this man, and I followed it up by actively hating him each day. Do you blame me? At the time I wouldn't have called it a grudge, though. I would have called it a normal human reaction, which it was. I didn't think hating him was bad, because he deserved it. What he'd done was wrong, and he knew it was wrong, but he still chose to do nothing about it. He didn't care about me or my family; he only cared about himself.

So I prepared my case and sent it to a lawyer who agreed to help me sue him. The lawyer took pity on me and handled my case without charging me a retainer. I wanted my business partner to be accountable. I wanted him to understand that leaving me with all the financial responsibility of a dying brokerage was wrong. I wanted him to feel the consequences as I had.

Both my husband and I were working sixteen to eighteen hours a day, trying to pay back all the debt, while trying to keep the lights on at home and food on the table. My lawyer tried to settle the claim without having to go to court, but my business partner never responded to his letter. Eventually my husband and I forgot about suing and figured that collecting any money was a lost cause. We moved on with life, thinking that we might as well get busy and pay it all back.

As time passed, we moved on with our lives, but at odd moments, rage and hatred would rear their ugly heads to remind us how ripped off and betrayed we felt. Two years later, we were still paying down the debt when, in September of 2010, I had my near-death experience. It was our belief that the overwhelming financial stress was the cause of my near-death experience. The trauma of this experience left me very physically sick, emotionally stunted, and spiritually confused. I was not able to physically work, which put an even larger financial strain on our already destitute world. This left my husband with even more hatred, rage, anger, resentment, and disgust for this man, which only further threatened what little was left of our relationship.

In Part One, I shared how acute my sensitivities were and that while I was learning to cope, I couldn't stand to be around my husband's energy. I am sure that now we can appreciate why. But this is what makes grudges so powerful and destructive. It becomes a vicious circle with no end. Grudges are powerfully destructive, not only for the one who is actively holding on to them, but also for all others caught in the ripple effect.

Several months after my near-death experience, my husband and I were severely struggling in our relationship and learning how to be together again. One day, to our surprise, a letter came from my lawyer informing us that, after nearly three years, they had finally been successful at serving my business partner, and that a court date was set to finalize this matter. We had thought it was over and forgotten. This was all we needed—as if we already didn't have enough on our plates!

I was now a different person, thinking in *alert consciousness* and feeling my own *spiritual energy*. I thought differently about this whole situation. I no longer had any thoughts of hatred or malice. There had been a lot of changes in almost three years. But my husband's viewpoint hadn't changed. He still hated my business partner, hated what he'd done to our family and was ecstatic at the thought of going to battle, and making him pay.

When your mind is in *alert consciousness*, your thoughts are clear and your intentions are based in love. It doesn't mean you just roll over and let people walk all over you. I no longer wanted to hurt this man or cause him and his family financial hardship such as we were suffering. In another year all of the debt would be cleared. The emotional disturbance of a court date and revisiting this situation would not be good for my SVT condition, my relationship with my husband, or for *my* highest good, because I was no longer the same person. It was not worth pursuing and I had no intention of re-opening this wound. It would be in my highest interest to just dismiss this claim.

If I had actively decided to sue my partner, it would *not* have been out of malice and revenge but common sense based in *alert consciousness*. I had come to the conclusion that since we were probably not going to resolve this issue, there was no use harbouring all this negativity. Why would I expend my great positive energy on a negative situation? Logically, why would I continue to throw good money after bad? Out of revenge, hatred, and anger? I felt it was not in my highest interest to continue with the lawsuit, but that decision was not acceptable to my husband. He definitely did not see it my way!

So now let's talk about the triggers. Can you see where we were constantly triggered? When I wasn't triggered, my husband was; and when he wasn't triggered, I was. So what did this do for us? It kept us in constant pain, anger, hatred, resentment, rage, and self-pity for a few years.

Why were we triggered? The demise of my relationship with my business partner left me feeling wronged, ripped off, deserted, abandoned, and forsaken. Because my husband loves me, he took on this pain also. The business closure *forced my husband* to pay off a lot of the residual debt, which amplified his anger and resentment.

To make matters worse, my husband and I were now struggling with the after-effects of my NDE, which we believed to be a direct result of the [original] lawsuit. Our financially destitute world, our terribly fragmented relationship, and my husband's emotional scars from watching me die that night were all triggers, and they kept coming fast and furious. Someone had to be responsible for all this pain!

The energy of a grudge is so powerfully negative, without our even knowing it. It's like a deadly silent disease being passed from one person to another, from one generation to the next. Worst of all, while we were so self-absorbed in hating this man, my son became a victim of our equally bad energy. He collected what I would call *residual energy;* no one can escape the ripple effect of residual bad energy. Grudges are a learned behaviour; they are not *instinctual*. Grudges are a character flaw. But, without grudges we could not learn forgiveness.

* * *

CHAPTER SIXTEEN

Forgiveness

What is forgiveness? Forgiveness is what we want when we make a mistake. We want an unconditional, loving pardon. We don't want our error in judgement to be brought up continually. We want a clean slate; we want a fresh start in order to do better. That, to me, is forgiveness. It is easy to think about forgiveness when it is something *we* want when *we* make a mistake. But, it's a lot harder to forgive when someone else has wronged *us*. Did you ever notice that?

When I have this conversation about forgiveness with others, they get defensive and tell me, "I forgive all the time; *that* is not one of my problems." But a few short breaths later they are still resentful, angry, frustrated, and hurt by that same person they've apparently forgiven. How is this?

Why do we want forgiveness? Forgiveness is an extension of love. It is an act of love. As love, trust, respect, and joy are important in our relationships, so is forgiveness. We need forgiveness to right the wrongs. We want forgiveness to restore balance in a relationship and to put us back on course. Forgiveness is the core of our *spiritual vibrational energy*;

and, in our *alert consciousness* we realize that grudges are of the body. We want to feel forgiveness so we can live happily with others and carry on with life.

Why should we forgive? We forgive because that is how we were created and that is how we grow relationships. Sometimes people are not able to forgive because their pain, anger, rage, bitterness, and resentment are insurmountable, and forgiveness seems too far out of reach.

We are an extension of our Divine Source, and when we make a mistake, the Divine Source forgives us. Therefore, we all know what it is to unconditionally forgive because we are Oneness. We *do* have it in us to forgive others, no matter what wrong has been done.

This only means that a fresh path between the two parties has been made. It doesn't mean that you will go back to engage in more wrongdoing. It also doesn't mean that a loving, nurturing relationship *must* now bloom. Forgiveness means that a clear understanding between two parties has cleaned the slate, abolishing all negative or harmful *residual energy*. In fact, you may not come into contact with this person again after the slate has been cleaned.

What if I can't forgive? We all have it within us to forgive. One main reason why forgiveness might not be obtainable is because not enough time has elapsed to heal the wound. Forgiveness is of our Divine Source and of us, but time is needed to heal the wound. Forgiveness can't be forced; it is a loving, unselfish act of *doing* when ready. If not enough time has passed to heal the wound, the act of forgiving can't happen. Forgiveness is not *forgetting* but *remembering* what to do for yourself, your brother, and for the greater good of Oneness. If you do not learn how to forgive, the original situation will repeat itself. That means wrongs will continually be done unto you, until you learn the lesson of Oneness, which is to forgive.

How do I forgive? Forgiveness is only one act of *undoing*. It doesn't matter if *you* are looking for forgiveness, or if someone else is looking *to you* for forgiveness. The act of forgiveness is the same unconditional, loving action of undoing and clearing the energy of a wrong. Time is needed; maybe a lot of time, maybe only minutes, but time is essential, as it can heal all wounds. The amount of time is different for each individual.

Forgiveness is a necessary growth factor for any relationship. Even if you never want to see or be around the person who wronged you, the act of forgiveness is a growth factor for the relationship with yourself! No special ritual needs to take place; perhaps no words to the other person even have to be said. Forgiveness is within you and your *spiritual vibrational energy*. It is shared with others through our body's *alert consciousness* state of mind.

Why do I have trouble forgiving? Sometimes the pain that we have suffered at the hands of someone else is so great that we don't want to forget. We seem to think that if we *forgive* then that means we need to *forget* that the pain ever existed. No, that is not the case. Grudges and forgiveness are linked in this way.

We hold grudges to remember the pain and then justify keeping our grudges in the name of justice or accountability, or for fear the other person will *get off easy*. Sometimes we just don't know *why* we should forgive or *how* we could forgive. But we always seem to be able to justify keeping the grudge!

We have trouble forgiving because we want those who have wronged us to feel our pain, anger, hostility, rage, or sadness, and if we were to *forgive* them then our pain would not be validated. Waiting for *those who wronged us* to validate our pain, may be a waste of *your* precious time. If it can't be validated, it doesn't mean that our pain won't go away. It means you will find forgiveness in a different way.

The act of forgiveness is one action, one unconditional, loving action, to clean the slate, start fresh; it is a loving action of *undoing*. With this, the negative destructive energy will disappear. *You* don't clear the energy; the act of forgiveness through our Divine Source clears the energy.

Although forgiveness is one act, it can have two parts to it: the apology and the acceptance of the apology. It is very important to apologize when mistakes are made, because the process of forgiveness then becomes easier. Conversely, accepting apologies and granting forgiveness is equally as important.

REMEMBER: An apology or acceptance of an apology *must* be authentic. If you are just going through the motions and providing lip service, your energy won't lie. This causes more damage than never apologizing, not only for you but also for the other person. If you are not ready or are unable to forgive them, you can accept their apology. Your inability to forgive is not their problem, but your choice and your own personal journey of pain.

If I can't access this person, can forgiveness still happen? In a perfect world, when a person is wronged by another, an authentic *apology* is offered, and in return they lovingly accept the apology and all the negative energy is cleared. However, we don't live in a perfect world, and people continually make mistakes.

If you have wronged someone and you want forgiveness, then you need to say you are sorry and ask for forgiveness. For whatever reason, if they are not ready and need more time, then you must allow that person the time they need to heal. If forgiveness is what you seek in order to strengthen your relationship and continue to grow it, then you must be patient while *they* heal the wound *you* created.

If you want forgiveness from a person you are now unable to reach, possibly because they have already died, you can still obtain forgiveness. It is in these situations that we must forgive ourselves. The forgiveness you will seek will be from your Divine Source. It is in seeking and asking that you will be forgiven, and the relationship with yourself and your Divine Source will be strengthened.

With time, the other person in the relationship may or may not be able to forgive. If, for whatever reason, they are not able to forgive, then the energy cannot be fully cleared, because they are still holding on to it. Their inability to forgive is their journey, not yours.

If you want to forgive someone who has wronged you and there is no possible way that they will validate your pain or ever offer anything authentic to you, then you need to focus on the relationship with yourself and your Divine Source. Sometimes when we have been wronged, our aggressors might not even know that they have hurt us, making it difficult for forgiveness or healing to take place. In this case, the aggressor needs to know and should be given the opportunity to make it right.

Hopefully, an apology will ensue, followed by an acceptance, and then forgiveness can begin. If our aggressor knows what they did and that it was wrong but chooses to do nothing about it, then you need to forgive them for the sake of your own relationship with yourself. Forgive them, because you need it more than they do.

In the case of my business partner, it took an NDE to make me understand forgiveness. It wasn't hard to forgive him; it was a lot harder to learn about the act of forgiving. Even though I might never see him again, I needed to forgive him because the anguish, rage, hostility, and hatred were boiling over inside me. The rippling effect of my negative emotions began to damage the relationship I had with all those around me. The suffering of holding on to this grudge prohibited forgiveness, which only harmed me and all those I was in a relationship with. Forgiveness was for me, but moreover, for him as well. In receiving it for myself I automatically granted it to him, whether he knew it or not. If he chooses to hold on to a grudge, that becomes his journey and not my responsibility.

Once I authentically forgave him, I no longer felt any negative energy toward him. This was not the case for my husband. The vicious circle of a grudge still remained for my husband. As I write this today, my husband is still struggling with forgiving this man, but I love my husband and I will wait patiently until this wound has healed. Then forgiveness will happen for him too.

Apologies are nice, validation of our hurt feelings is wonderful, but we don't live in a perfect world where this may happen. But with time, it does become your responsibility to find forgiveness for those who've wronged you, to grow and develop your relationship with the Divine Source and with yourself.

* * *

CHAPTER SEVENTEEN

Giving and Trying

*L*et's talk about the difference between giving and trying. One definition of giving is "to freely transfer the possession of something to someone; hand over to."

Before my NDE, I felt that I was a very giving person. I volunteered and organized golf tournaments to raise money for sick children that took a lot of time and work. I gave financial donations to the blind and food banks, and donated often to shelters. I gave all that I had to my son while he was growing, I was with my dad every waking hour for several months before his death, and I helped all those around me even when I really couldn't or didn't want to.

If you had told me back then that I was only *trying* but not actually *giving*, I would have been very offended and hurt and you probably would have triggered a pronounced, defensive reaction. I probably would have told you that I didn't *try*; I GAVE. If we've learned anything so far about triggers it's that there must be some truth to the thoughts that have triggered us, or else we wouldn't have been triggered.

Since my NDE and living in *spiritual consciousness*, my view on giving is totally different. Another one of our triggers is the *perception* of *giving*.

Everyone has a different perception of what *giving* really means. Think about what *giving* means to you right now. Take a moment and really think about it. Before moving on, write down on a piece of paper some of the things that you have done, and what you would consider *giving* is.

Now let me share with you my version of giving, since living in spiritual consciousness and having a Choir. {*Giving is doing without any thought about getting in return; giving is done without complaining during or after; giving is when you can, not when you think you should; giving is the act of love and done in your highest good; giving is innocent; giving is within the intention of your spiritual vibrational energy.*}

Some examples of giving: When you are out shopping and notice that someone has dropped their glove and they don't know it, you stop and pick it up to hand it back. They usually say thank you—leaving you feeling pretty good. When your next-door neighbour's husband dies, you bake a pan of lasagne and take it over to her. Your buddy's car breaks down so you give him a lift to work the next day. A friend wants to borrow one of your tools. When an earthquake strikes, you gather all your old clothes to donate them. Giving is innocent, without thought, without complaint, without the thought of getting anything back in return, without any hopes of reciprocation.

CAUTION: This next part may trigger some readers because the thought that their idea of *giving* was really only *disguised trying* can be uncomfortable to process and challenging to our egos. As I said earlier, if you'd had this conversation with me before my NDE, I would have been hurt, offended, and probably in denial and triggered to be defensive and angry. Where there is a trigger, there is truth.

Let's talk about the opposite of *giving*. Do you know what that is? Some may say *taking* or *getting*, because if you are not giving then you must be taking.

What we are talking about here is only half giving; and if it's only half then it is not really giving anymore, is it? It's kind of like being half-pregnant: that state really doesn't exist either. You are either pregnant or you are not. Like being half-pregnant, half-giving doesn't exist either. You are either giving or just *trying*.

Now let's look at *trying*. There are many definitions for trying, depending on how it is used. In this instance, my definition of *trying* is {*an intention to attempt willingly or unwillingly to perform an action knowing that failure is an acceptable option where the outcome may or may not be beneficial to me*}.

The major difference between *giving* and *trying* is the attempt or intention, its origin, and whether you complain while doing it. With *giving*, the intention is innocent and without thinking. In *trying*, thoughts of reciprocation might be present. *Giving's* origin is of *spiritual vibrational energy* and *trying* is of your yappy *mindless consciousness*, which becomes triggered if your intentions are challenged. Giving is done innocently and without thought or complaint, while *trying* is riddled with voiced complaints or silent thoughts of whining.

Some examples of *trying* to give: Giving charitable donations to non-profit organizations in exchange for a receipt that will be of benefit at tax time; volunteering long hours organizing golf tournaments to raise money for sick children, only to complain during or after the event; raising a family while resenting the sacrifice you must make. *Trying* is cooking a Christmas meal for your family when you really didn't want to, then pretending it was your highest joy as they eat it. Helping someone when you really don't want to, but feeling pressure to do so. Spending time with a loved one who is in hospice but being preoccupied with fear that they will be gone soon.

Don't get me wrong, *trying* is still good; it's great. Charities need donations, loved ones dying in hospice need family, sacrifices must be made when raising children, and we all do things for others when we really can't or just don't want to. I want to caution you that it is not called *giving*, it is called *trying*; and there is nothing wrong with *trying*. Sometimes that is all we have to offer. *The trigger comes in when you tell someone you are giving when your body language and energy says you are trying.*

The purpose of this section is to understand triggers and where they come from. *Giving* will never activate a trigger; however, *trying* will activate a trigger, but only when you try to convince someone it is *giving*. The trigger will be hurt, pain, sadness, betrayal, confusion, avoidance, and despair or depression. If someone tries to hold you accountable for *trying* and not *giving*, then your trigger will be anger, defensiveness, guilt, and avoidance.

So there you have it, my version of triggers as they played havoc with my life and in my relationships. I still get triggered today, but not as often as I used to. Triggers will only go away with honesty ... brute honesty. My hope is that baring my soul to you with complete honesty will help you to do the same for *yourself*. You do not have to share your honesty with anyone. This is your journey to find out who you are, not who you wish you would be.

Honesty is the key to an easier journey of self-discovery. These were probably the hardest chapters I had to write, as I had to re-live some of my intimate triggers. Although it was the most healing part of my journey, it was by far the most difficult time in my life to get through. It is through the lack of love and the viciousness of mankind that we can learn. It feels great to learn, but the lessons themselves can be awfully painful.

It is within this chapter's pages that we can recognize the warnings, acknowledge our feelings, and take responsibility for choosing or not choosing to change our perceptions. My painful journey to understanding triggers doesn't have to be yours. Any time we try to understand new concepts, or dig deep into self-discovery, we can be confronted with challenges. But I promise you, even recognizing one small trigger will forever alter your life for the better.

I hope you enjoyed these chapters and that they helped show you why we *all* get triggered and the source of some of these triggers. The next chapter is the final follow-through to understanding that *ALL* of our triggers *originated* from *only one root, only one starting point*. Now we can come full circle in understanding triggers. Triggers are the debris in your drain. Locate the root of *all* your triggers and unclog your drain! The journey of life is wonderful and filled with beautiful surprises, but no one said it would be easy. After all, we are spiritual beings enjoying a *human experience.*

* * *

CHAPTER EIGHTEEN

Root of All Triggers

*I*n this chapter, we will complete the circle and find out where our guilt, fear, grudges, anger, judgment, and lack of self-worth originated. This chapter will tie up a lot of loose ends and fill in any gaps; if you are still unclear, go back and re-read some chapters. There is a lot to process and digest; it is like learning to walk all over again. Spiritual growth is unlike textbook learning; it takes time, patience, understanding, and practicing being aware.

Let's begin with a little recap of what we've learned so far.

After reviewing some of the painful reactions that triggers can bring, we now find ourselves moving out of recognizing and more into practicing. We know that all triggers were created by the yappy side of our mind, or our *mindless consciousness*. In the beginning, recognizing negative triggers is the easiest. The interactions we have with people are called relationships. In a relationship, the other person may unknowingly provoke us to feel a powerful reaction such as anger, rage, or sadness, and this provocation is called a *trigger*. If you get triggered, it is your responsibility to recognize and accept your trigger. Do not blame the other person for your provoked emotion. When triggered, *you* own the emotion, not them. Instead, consider your trigger a gift from them. Think of it as if they are helping you to clear all your triggers and unplug your drain!

Conversely, we may unknowingly and innocently provoke a trigger in someone else. Do not take responsibility for *their* trigger. They will not want to feel this trigger, so they will try to hold you accountable for their pain. If it is their pain, it's their trigger, and then it becomes their responsibility.

The gage of our triggers is our emotions, which are based within our self-worth, guilt, validation, self-confidence, judgment, fear, and/or grudges. So where did these emotions come from? If we can find the root of our problems, then our triggers will be minimized and all of our relationships and interactions with other people will have no choice but to flourish.

There is only one root to ALL of the negative emotions. The root is called *Ego*. Slowly, and in great detail, we will walk through this together. For me, the two most debilitating sources of my triggers were my lack of self-worth, which I demonstrated in my journal writing, and my sense of not being *normal*, which was based in fear. But each negative emotion is just as debilitating as the next, so I have briefly dissected many sources so you can see the commonality among them. The most important fact is that *ALL* emotional triggers come from only *ONE* root, and that is *EGO!*

ALL TRIGGERS BEHAVING LIKE ONE

SOURCE OF TRIGGER: Lack of self-worth; Fear; Grudges; Judgmentalism; Need for validation from others; Lack of self-confidence; Lack of self-esteem; Guilt.

ROOT: Ego: The root of all triggers.

POSSIBLE REASON FOR TRIGGER: Lack of sense of true identity; an event or a situation that contradicts or challenges one's perceived sense of individual identity or safety.

POSSIBLE CAUSE OF TRIGGER: Sense of security is challenged, destroyed, or lost. Past abuse by a person of trust; Past manipulation by a person of trust; Disability; Loss of status; Loss of income; Loss of possessions; Loss of independence.

POSSIBLE REACTION TO TRIGGER: Anger; Frustration; Anxiety; Sadness; Resentment; Hatred; Worry; Hurt feelings; Avoidance.

POSSIBLE VICTIMS OF TRIGGER: Everyone and everything the individual may perceive to be less than or better than himself. Hence, anyone.

Targets typically perceived by ego as *less than*: The homeless, prostitutes, renters, waitress, janitorial staff, some races, our children, poor neighbourhoods, old beaten-down cars, unattractive people, overweight people, people with disabilities, etc.

Targets perceived by ego as *better than*: Anyone perceived to have more intelligence, wisdom, relationships, status, good looks, money, possessions, fame, or love.

POSSIBLE LIFE OUTCOME: "Wanna Be." To act out the persona you think you *should be*; or try to become who you think you might *want to be*, or who *others want you to be*.

What is Ego?

So what is ego and where does it belong? Is it a *source* of our pain or a *trigger* when we feel pain? Well, it is both. Ego is the root of all sources of pain. Ego is the only part of us that is really triggered.

Wow! Feel that for a moment. Yes, ego is everything! Ego is the root of all of our pain, and it is the only trigger mechanism that we feel when we interact with others. Although the emotions of anger, fear, hurt feelings, and frustration are exhibited, they are only *symptoms* of ego. When relationships experience difficulties there is a clash of egos; either our ego is getting in the way or the other person's is. This is why we can work easily with some people and can't stand to be around others. This is why we automatically feel connected to some while repelling or being repelled by others.

So what really is ego? My Choir's description of ego is {*an energetic state of being we created within our yappy mindless consciousness which we developed out of pain; slowly losing our true sense of self by tuning out our alert consciousness thereby, disabling our spiritual consciousness making it impossible to hear or feel any messages being sent from our Divine Source*}. Now *that* is a mouthful!

Let's break that down and take a moment to recap what *spiritual consciousness* is. Born within every human being is a *spiritual vibrational energy* which is incapable of dying, and is waiting to go back to the spirit world. *Alert consciousness,* which is the opposite of the yappy side of the mind, connects to our *spiritual vibrational energy*, which allows us to hear or feel messages from our Divine Source, loved ones who have passed on, or our angels. The *state of being* while receiving messages from our *spiritual vibrational energy* through the alert side of the mind is called *spiritual consciousness.*

The ONLY obstacle that prohibits us from *spiritual consciousness* is EGO! The fact that ego has disabled our *spiritual consciousness* doesn't mean that the communication link to our Divine Source and Angels no longer exists. In fact, the line of communication is ever-powerful and patiently waiting for you to figure out that it has been disabled. For the time being it is only temporarily out of order.

This is much like the previous telephone line and receiver analogy. Right now you have a perfectly functioning, open line of communication between you and your Divine Source, but your telephone receiver, *alert consciousness*, has been temporarily disabled by ego. It is not broken, only disabled!

So let's look at the same chart again with a few minor changes showing what ego is, where it comes from, and why it is here.

WHAT IS EGO?

WHAT IS EGO: Pain
ROOT: Mindless Consciousness
REASON FOR EGO: Lack of True Identity
CAUSE OF EGO: Life Experiences
RESULT OF EGO: Disables Spiritual Consciousness
EGO'S TRIGGER: Fear
EGO'S VICTIMS: All Relationships
A LIFE OUTCOME WITH EGO: Unfulfilled; Searching for True Self

We are solely responsible for creating and developing ego. Ego development began when we were children learning the difference between *our kind* and *their kind*. It began with a fantasy that we were a prince or princess, or that we were rich and famous, or that we were mommies and daddies playing house. Never did we imagine and fantasize about living in poverty, prostituting our bodies, starving, and living on the streets with no roof over our head! That is a choice, the same choice as creating ego.

Ego was further developed as we went through school acting as a bully or being bullied, being a good student or a rebellious one. All of our experiences develop and shape our ego. For example, the ego of a bully is going to be different from that of his bullied victim. Nevertheless, both people, although different, have ego, but experiences have just developed it differently. As ego grows and thrives, our *spiritual consciousness* becomes smothered. At this point we are able to still feel our *spiritual vibrational energy*—but just barely.

Ego development expanded greatly as we approached adulthood, when we got ourselves in and out of trouble, accomplished great things, and began entering into and terminating committed relationships. This further expansion as adults holds ego tightly in place. It becomes so fixed in our yappy *mindless consciousness* that we have temporarily disabled our *spiritual consciousness*. The difficulty is that ego has been here for *so long* that we don't even know that *spiritual consciousness* exists. Ego has created the illusion of such a wonderful, safe, comfortable place within our yappy *mindless consciousness* that it is unfathomable to think that another part exists. It is almost impossible to perceive that there are two parts to our mind. Good job, ego!

Many people have the perception that ego is associated with affluence. Poor people don't have ego? We all have ego, some different than others, but we all have ego. Imagine, as your ego has been created and developed in your life, so too is that same ego wreaking havoc within everyone else's; they are no better or no worse. That is why it is important to first recognize ego and its triggers in you because ego will then become discernable in others.

It is only when we can see another's ego that we can separate their *spiritual vibrational energy* from their physical being called the body. In separating the ego from spirit you will feel the outside triggered energy but will also feel the loving *spiritual vibrational energy*.

If ego is wreaking that much havoc in all our lives, how do we get rid of ego? And, if we do get rid of ego, then all of our collective problems are solved ... right?

* * *

CHAPTER NINETEEN

Get Rid
of Ego?

*W*e actually don't want to get rid of ego! Ego teaches us about *spiritual consciousness*, teaches us to feel and hear again, and teaches us everything we need to learn about love and forgiveness. Ego is our freedom. Let me explain.

When I was leaving the hospital on the night of my NDE, I felt so alive, filled with love for everyone, including myself. My mind was firing on all cylinders, I was excited, I could see better, hear better, and sense and know as I had when I was dead. But when I got home, the *old reality and routine* set right in. The new Lorri couldn't function in the old Lorri's world. That is when the separation of ego from *spiritual consciousness* unknowingly began. So how did that happen?

My old yappy *mindless consciousness* was disconnected for a few days after I got home. I lived in the moment, being *spiritually conscious,* receiving unfathomable messages from our Divine Source and my loved ones who had passed on. It was a wonderful time—brief, but wonderful.

Then the *reality* of the *old* Lorri's life—the financial ruin, hating my business partner, fearing that I wasn't normal—kicked in hard and disabled *spiritual consciousness.* This period of confusion, anger, and depression drove me to thoughts of ending it all because I had very few coping skills. It was like being in Heaven one minute, and then back to financial ruin and hate the next ... Who *wouldn't* want to leave?

Then a few days later, *spiritual consciousness* would reconnect, offering love, answers, wisdom, support, joy, happiness, and peace. It would last for a couple of weeks until something triggered me. Usually my trigger was not being *normal*. When paranormal things would happen that weren't *normal* in the old Lorri's life, then I would start to panic, worry, feel low self-esteem and self-confidence, and experience sadness.

Let's talk about sadness for a moment. I never knew what depression was or felt anything like it before my NDE. But the sadness I felt was gut-wrenching and horribly painful. I cried continually, and within this sadness I couldn't see hope anymore. I desperately didn't want to feel this engulfing sadness any longer I knew I had to do something, but I never knew what. This type of extreme sadness was not *normal* for the *old* Lorri, which again reinforced the notion that I was *not normal*, which triggered me further into *mindless consciousness*. I began to be my own worst trigger.

As I sit here writing this I can honestly say that if I had known *how* to change my state of mind, I suspect my recovery would have been drastically shorter and not as painful. This is why I am sharing all that I know with you today: I want the horrible pain I felt to be put to good use in helping others. If you can understand this level of sadness then please know that it *can* be brief and *can* be eliminated.

After a few weeks of insane depression, anger, fear, and loneliness, something would happen: peace, joy, and love would reconnect and be back in an instant. I never knew what triggered these blissful moments, but I prayed that they would *stay*. Then an overdue invoice would come to the house, my husband's energy would be horrible, my trigger of not feeling normal, or just the cruelty of day-to-day life would kick in. Then *spiritual consciousness* was temporarily out of service again and it was back to the same old pain, the same *old Lorri*. The feeling of amazing peace, love, health, and spiritual wholeness that *spiritual consciousness* had brought would be wiped away instantaneously and without warning, leaving anger and depression in its wake.

This roller coaster of emotions lurched from one total extreme to the other, like poverty at one end of a spectrum and fortune at the other. This made life really difficult for my husband, my family, and me.

My journey didn't have to be that painful; I made it that way. Although I suffered a painful journey, now there is not a day that passes since finding *spiritual consciousness* that I am not grateful, and I will be forever happy that I had *ego* to thank for all of this! Without ego triggering me, how would I come to know that I didn't want it? How could I possibly have found out that there is another side to my mind? How could I have felt *spiritual consciousness*?

Today, I have a clear understanding as to why I would flip from blissful moments of peaceful, loving communication and wisdom to the dankness of anger, suicidal thoughts, and fear. It was because of ego. Everything happens for a reason, and ego has a purpose. The purpose of ego is to teach you how to become *spiritually conscious*!

Ego shows us joy by first showing us pain. Without feeling pain, how would you know what joy feels like? Ego shows us peace through anger, aggression, and hostility. Ego shows us love, but first shows us hatred. Every day ego shows us the first part of our lesson, which is anger, aggression, hostility, fear, hatred, etc. Our *spiritual energy*, through *alert consciousness*, teaches us the second part of our lesson. Ego shows us, while *spiritual consciousness* teaches us. Our Divine Source gave us choices, and now it's up to us to choose if we want to learn the lessons.

My painful learning period lasted more than nine months! My experience of a NDE was a blessing because my recovery showed me *spiritual consciousness*. Ego showed me unbearable pain. Am I more grateful for the NDE than for the presence of my ego? Of course not, because without the opposite of love and peace within *spiritual consciousness*, how could I ever have known that two sides actually existed? Without an

NDE, how do we know that an afterlife or Heaven exists? If we were only to feel joy and never feel any pain, could the joy really be appreciated?

Gratitude cannot exist without its opposite. If our life was only perfectly happy or perfectly peaceful, how would we ever know a Divine Source? It is in times of ego manifestation that we find ourselves searching for peace. So without pain we would not know peace; with only peace and no pain we would not come to know our Divine Source.

That is why, my friend, we need ego. We need pain and havoc in order to find the other peaceful side of loving spiritual communication with our Divine Source and all the Angels! We have been shown where some of our triggers are coming from so we can come to easily recognize what they may feel like. We also know that ego is the root of all our painful triggers, such as lack of self-worth, fear, grudges, judgmentalism, etc.

So what is the root of ego? Ego was created within the yappy *mindless consciousness*, but what is *ego's* root? The root of ego is our Divine Source! Yup ... it shocked me, too! Why would our Divine Source do such a cruel thing to us? Actually, though, it is a *gift*, a special gift to us.

Without the freedom to choose to develop your ego you would not be the individual you are today. Everyone would be the same. You wouldn't know love because you wouldn't know hatred. You wouldn't know peace because you wouldn't know pain. And *we* wouldn't know Heaven if there was no death. So when you feel triggered by one of your brothers, know that it is from our Divine Source and it's a gift, not a curse!

It is in that *moment in time* that our Divine Source is giving you the opportunity to see love, peace, and an afterlife, and is giving you the opportunity to choose. The tool our Divine Source uses is ego, and it is used within the loving context of relationships. So when ego's trigger surfaces, try to find gratitude in that you have an opportunity to feel and hear your Divine Source, try to find peace in that this is exactly what is meant to happen, and decide freely what you want to do with this opportunity. No matter what you decide to do, our Divine Source will continue to use His tool of ego and triggers in relationships so you may always know the love of Oneness and of our Divine Source.

So why does this lesson have to be learned with the ones I love? What about harmony and love within relationships? Well, that is exactly why ego was created. The painful triggers we feel happen mostly with the people we have chosen to love. The pain of triggers needs to be loud so you can wake up and hear the message. If the trigger were quiet, what purpose would that serve?

The whole purpose to our existence is relationships, so the lesson becomes more powerful when it is done within a relationship you chose out of love, does it not? Would you get the same effect with a perfect stranger? Probably not. The purpose of pain is to teach the lesson and strengthen relationships. It is by your choice that you are *not* learning the lesson. In denying ego you deny the lesson. In denying the lesson, you deny a relationship with your Divine Source.

So now we know why we have ego, what caused ego, what its root is, and why we need it. Lastly, we will figure out how to use ego to find *spiritual consciousness*, peace, and love. It is a very, very simple process that will come naturally and automatically.

* * *

CHAPTER TWENTY

Tips for an Easier Journey

Recognizing your ego will show you that two sides of your mind exist and that a separation is possible. As fleeting moments of *spiritual consciousness* shine through your days, you will enjoy *spiritual consciousness* much better than ego.

There might be some frustration when ego creeps in more than you would like. Some days it might feel as if you are nothing *but* ego, which is perfect too. It is in seeing ego that you recognize that ego exists. Becoming aware of ego's existence and *knowing* that you are *seeing* ego is all that you need to do. The rest will fall perfectly into place.

To me, ego is like a stinkweed and your *alert consciousness* is like a beautiful garden. If you don't keep picking the weed it will soon take over the entire garden. If your garden is already overgrown, then more time, patience, and love may be required to pick out the weed in order to let the sun back in.

There will be days when you no sooner pick the weed than it will be right back again. This might make you angry or frustrated, but let me reassure you, the weed is much more threatened about being picked than you are frustrated that you have to do it again and again. Keep picking, don't quit.

You have a beautiful garden. It isn't dead or gone; it's just overrun! So take joy in weeding your garden every minute of each day and watch it bloom more gloriously than you could have imagined! Soon the weeds of ego won't come back. And know that I am sending you love and blessings while you weed and grow your wonderful garden.

As you begin *your* journey of recognizing and practicing removing triggers, I would like to give you some tips so you can make your journey pleasant, as mine was painful.

1. OPEN MIND: Be open to the possibility that the mind has two parts to it. The night I died, I went in as one person but came out another. My body was exactly the same but my mind was totally different ... therefore I experienced two parts to the mind. In the beginning, while testing this stuff out, your mind will become more open as you start to see both parts working.

2. RECOGNIZE A TRIGGER: Understand that a trigger is a threatened ego. Anytime a threat is present a trigger will occur. The cause of a trigger is *emotional pain* ... that's it! But the pain is very real, which leads us to the need for validation.

3. VALIDATE: Celebrate that you were triggered! This means that you can see ego; not everyone does. The most important part here is to validate the pain you feel is *your ego*. Believe me, I know the pain is real. Whether it is anger, hurt feelings, sadness, or frustration—it is very real. Validate this raw emotion in that moment and accept that it is the pain of ego only. This pain is real and here for a reason. Truly, it has a meaningful purpose and is not meant solely to upset you or those around you.

4. CHOOSE: Choose what you are going to do with this pain. You have two choices. You can accept that it has meaning even though you may not know what that meaning is right now. Or, you can reject it and let it go and pretend it doesn't bother you, and continue harbouring resentment and grudges. You get to choose to learn from the very real pain of triggers or pretend they don't exist and avoid them at all costs.

5. RECOGNIZE THAT YOU RECOGNIZED: This is the *Shift* and it's the easiest step of all. It is so easy that we tend to forget it altogether. This part is the only part that keeps us in *alert consciousness*, gets us closer to clear communication with our Divine Source, and allows us to find *spiritual consciousness*. In other words, this part is like already having your arm in the drain of your dirty water, finding and grabbing a huge piece of debris, but pulling your arm out with nothing in your hand! Grab that piece of debris and empty your drain! If you forget to *Shift* then the trigger will keep re-surfacing. Now that I've reminded you that this step exists and that it's critically important—always remember this important step ... please!

I was Triggered and I Accepted it. What do I do now?

Let's be clear: triggers will happen whether you like it or not. Triggers will happen when you least want them or least expect them. Triggers erupt from the actions of people you might least expect to trigger you. If you have tested anything that I have said, I am sure that by now you must have recognized yourself being triggered by someone. Now the question becomes, what do I do with the trigger? How do I make the pain go away?

You have chosen to learn from ego, so what does that mean exactly? Ego is errors, and ego is incorrect perceptions. It is a *huge waste of time* trying to figure out where this pain came from (e.g., your past, your fear, your guilt, your lack of self-worth, etc). Really, it is. It will drive you crazy ... trust me! Even if you *may think* you *know* where your pain comes from, the pain will not go away. In fact, analyzing it only fuels the fire within your yappy *mindless consciousness*.

While we are analyzing where this pain is coming from we are filled with misunderstandings and false perceptions. While in ego and analyzing the pain, your false perception and false truth will usually find self-justification and push blame onto others. Can you see that by analyzing ego's pain, it's really ego justifying itself, which only feeds ego? That is why it is so hard to do very little. Our Divine Source made it so simple that it feels so difficult. Just recognize the trigger as ego's pain ... and then pat yourself on the back for recognizing it! That's it ... nothing more ... that's the lesson.

It might be very clear to you where this pain came from and why it has triggered you, but it still would be an illusion of your own perception. Most times we will not have any idea where this trigger is coming from, but it doesn't matter. Ego is the pain. For whatever reason, your triggered ego became threatened when confronted and pain appeared. It is *NOTHING* more than that.

This becomes the hard part, and do you know why? Because the yappy *mindless consciousness* needs an answer. It needs to know why; it desperately searches for the reason. There is no possible reason for ego's pain, which is a trigger, because ego is errors and perceptions capable only of non-truth.

The more you search for non-truth and hold on to resentment and anger, the more you feed your yappy *mindless consciousness*. Only *spiritual consciousness* is capable of wisdom, love, and forgiveness.

Recognizing the pain of ego is hard enough, but right now that is all you need to do. Once you can see that your painful trigger is your own ego acting up, then validate it by recognizing *that you recognized it*. That is it! If you give it any more thought and energy than that, you will be feeding ego. Remember, ego is a tool to help you obtain *spiritual consciousness* and recognize its false perceptions, errors, and non-truths.

All you need to do is recognize that you recognize. The ego you created is the same ego that I created. That's it. You don't have to do anything else. The rest will be done perfectly for you by our Divine Source. It will come naturally, I promise. It worked for me, it will for you!

* * *

PART THREE

3

Celebrating Life

CHAPTER ONE

Life's True Purpose

Your present circumstances don't determine where you can go;
they merely determine where you start.

~Nido Qubein

My sharing of *my* journey with you is almost over, but *our* journey *together* is just beginning! The last part of this book is called "Celebrating Life." And this is what I continue to do ... celebrate it with you! If you have reached this part, it means that you have probably encountered some pretty amazing epiphanies of your own!

So what does living your life's true purpose *mean*? How *many* true life purposes can there be? Which *one* is right? A definition of *purpose* is basically *the object for which something exists or is done.* Some books will tell you that your purpose is to be successful, happy, or prosperous, while others may indicate that your purpose is to give back, donate, or volunteer. Another group of books will tell you to cherish, live in gratitude, and honour your Divine Source because this will make you happy, prosperous, and healthy! Wow, they all seem to have a different idea as to what purpose is.

In *Heaven Time*, I am not saying that any of these is wrong or right. I am merely stating that having *purpose* is very subjective.

My *old purpose* was to live ethically, morally, and spiritually the best way I could with the hope that good karma would shine down upon me and bless me with health, happiness, and prosperity. Now, since my NDE and living in *spiritual consciousness*, my purpose is totally different because my concept of *consciousness* is totally different. My definition of *purpose* is *{being how you were created}; sounds simple enough. So *what* was I *created* to do?

Purpose does not reside in a job, career, money, house, children, donating, volunteering, God, Divine Source, Heaven, or afterlife. Purpose is not right or wrong, successful or not successful. Purpose is not *doing*. Purpose is *being*. It is within that *being* that you will have a job, family, and fellowship. It is within that *being* that you will experience health, happiness, and financial freedom. The choice is yours.

What is my true purpose? I believe that we are amazing creatures with two exhilarating purposes. Remember, my version of purpose is *{being how you were created}*. As I have said numerous times, our *being* is made up of two parts, first a divine, all-knowing and powerful spirit, and then a physical body. So that would mean that we have two purposes that must come from our body and our spirit, respectively.

PURPOSE OF THE BODY: Our body's purpose is to listen and feel the divine messages through *spiritual consciousness* while growing and developing relationships. Its physical purpose is to cover our *spiritual vibrational energy*, acting as a protective shell that has a limited shelf life! Imagine for a moment that you have a rare baseball that was signed by Babe Ruth, or a priceless Faberge Egg. How would *you* take care of it? You would probably build a beautiful display case, shroud it in velvet, or put it into a vault, but you would never leave it on a cupboard to get broken or damaged, would you?

Well, that display case or vault is your body, which is protecting your *spiritual vibrational energy*. This is why there seem to be three purposes for our physical body. One is to protect our body, to keep it safe and healthy so the Divine Source can use it as a tool of communication. Another purpose is to procreate with other *spiritual vibrational energies*. And lastly, the body's mind has a purpose, which is to learn *alert consciousness*, allowing us to live in *spiritual consciousness* so we may develop and grow relationships with our Divine Source, others, and ourselves; all of this will strengthen Oneness. This is, in my opinion, what our body is for. So please treat it like the temple it is!

PURPOSE OF THE SPIRIT: Our *spiritual vibrational energy* has two purposes. First, and most important, it's the existence that we exist in! Our very existence reminds us that we were *all* conceived with an open line of *direct communication* with our Divine Source so that our bodies may hear and feel the messages that are being sent to us. Its second purpose is to provide us everlasting life so we may live on forever in the love of our Divine Source. Therefore, as human beings, our spiritual purpose is to find our *spiritual consciousness*, allowing us to feel the spiritual *vibrational energy* of others. This is so we can develop and grow *our individual spiritual vibrational energy* and strengthen our relationship with our Divine Source so we may live on forever in the essence of who we truly are.

Basically *being how you were created* means finding *spiritual consciousness*, which is your true physical and spiritual purpose. A job, money, possessions, children, poverty, happiness, sadness, grief are all components that come into play while you are on your search for *spiritual consciousness*.

WHAT SHOULD I DO WITH MY LIFE? If we can agree that the meaning of our life is finding *spiritual consciousness*, then the path your life takes really doesn't matter, because all paths will lead you to *spiritual consciousness, providing* this is what *you've chosen*.

Your job, the money you make, the possessions you have, the relationships you are in, or the number of children you conceive are directly related to your hope, happiness, sadness, self-worth, self-confidence, guilt, grief, and sense of security. These can be stumbling blocks and road barriers or they can be stepping stones and accomplishments; either way they are still paths to *spiritual consciousness*.

What you do with your life is your choice. The *search* for the *meaning of life* comes in when your sense of *self* is connected to job, money, fame, power, greed, or sadness. Instead, your sense of *self* should be connected to your Divine Source. Once your self is connected to your Divine Source and Oneness, it really doesn't matter *what* you do, but *how* you do it.

Your sense of daily purpose will be in the growth and development of relationships, while recognizing ego, feeling pain, and learning forgiveness. This is ultimately the meaning of love. So whether you clean houses, pick up garbage, are rich and famous, are homeless, financially destitute or grief-stricken with the loss of a loved one, it is not the *what* you are doing but *how* you are living in life that matters. The *spiritual vibrational energy* that is contained within each one of us is bursting to be seen and felt.

Before my NDE, I used to think that if I didn't give back in some way then I was greedy, and the law of karma would spite me. I felt emotionally fulfilled when I was helping people buy and sell houses because I thought they valued my service. However, my clients never *valued my service*, they *valued me*. Until I learned about *spiritual vibrational energy*, I realized, *I never valued me* in the way my clients did. They saw something in me that I *never saw*.

Knowing what I know now, it doesn't matter *what* we do with our lives as long as we do it in *spiritual consciousness*. It is in *spiritual consciousness* that our relationships flourish. It is here that we can separate ego from *spiritual vibrational energy*, a man from his actions, hate from love, and grudges from forgiveness.

So what do *I* do for work? I am no longer a real estate agent, but I do have a job that I am passionate about. It pays the bills, but my job doesn't define me; I define it! Today, I am a spiritual being named Lorri who openly shares her *spiritual consciousness* with everyone, hopefully raising the world's vibrational level just a little each time.

* * *

CHAPTER TWO

Living in Balance

When the power of love
overcomes the love of power,
the world will know peace.

~*Sri Chinmoy Ghose*

Y ou can be in balance while living in organized chaos. At this moment in time, my husband and I are in the middle of another move. Life is crazy. My husband is working long hours, I am working on my real estate website called *Soldplicity* and writing every chance I get, I have a full-time job, *and* I am preparing public seminars to continue sharing what I know. In my spare time I am packing and slowly moving, while setting up our other home. So life around here is pretty hectic and I can be triggered easily if I don't pay attention.

There are triggers around me all day long while I arrange for the moving company, utility companies, my work, the process of publishing this book, and my husband's crazy schedule. So how do you stay balanced, living in *spiritual consciousness*? It is very simple. Daily activities help you to *recognize* that you are recognizing. It doesn't matter what you are doing! Whether it's yoga, inspirational music and tapes, meditation, fishing, exercise, baking or cooking, volunteering, spending time with your special relationships, playing with your children, working on the car in your garage, or spending time with your parents or other elders. These are some activities that could be used to *ground* yourself and help reconnect your *alert consciousness*.

Living in balance *is practicing* being in *alert consciousness* for as many moments of the day as you can. The next day, try to be in even more moments. Before you know it, all the moments in your day are in *alert consciousness*. Without realizing it, one day you will be *continually* in *spiritual consciousness* and won't be able to explain how you got there! Becoming *spiritually conscious* isn't like a sneeze that happens fast. It's more like paint drying. One second it is still wet, and then gradually we can hang a picture! *Spiritual consciousness* will be gradual, without notice, *not* an abrupt *aha* moment.

Living in balance is practicing *to recognize*, within each action, every moment of your day. It doesn't matter if you can't do it right away, it only matters that you try. So why do we keep coming back for more, even if it hurts? It's very simple. It's for the love within relationships and to try to remember all that which we've forgotten. That's what our human existence is all about ... relationships. It is here that I want to thank you for *our* relationship. I am grateful that you've trusted my writing and validated my pain by giving it meaning. In return, I was honoured to intimately share my life and my experiences with you.

Do you remember the broken relationship of hatred I had for my business partner? Through *spiritual consciousness* I found forgiveness in that relationship because I believed he would *never* recognize or validate my pain. Let me share a little update with you. While finishing this book a court date was set to finalize this matter.

My husband was not in the mood to forgive or forget. I feared that the emotional disturbance of a court date and re-visiting this situation would only rip open a wound that, most likely, would *trigger* my husband.

Then the ripple effect of his painful trigger would also do harm to me and our relationship.

I, however, felt forgiveness, peace, and a sense of resolution toward my business partner, but the *residual* bad energy and pain from my husband was still plaguing our relationship. I no longer needed my pain to be validated, nor did I need or want any apologies. The only reason I continued with the process was because it was called *mediation*, which meant re*solution* to me. The only solution I was seeking was the hope of terminating the pain that my husband continued to hold on to, which slowly continued to deteriorate our relationship.

On the day of mediation, I was looking forward to seeing my business partner again. Although I felt happy and hopeful, I was sick to my stomach with nerves, worried that mediation would only rip open my husband's wound of anger and resentment. A mediation process consists of three parties around a table: two mediators, the plaintiff, and the defendant. It was presented very well.

We each began sharing our side of the story, which I think was beneficial for my husband to see, hear, and feel. For so many years we'd made my business partner the bad guy; we'd even made him responsible for my NDE! There were tears and sadness, but also laughter.

Upon looking at his side of the story, I realized that I am equally responsible. But more importantly, my husband got to *see* and *feel* the whole picture, and it became an opportunity for him to get rid of his anger and resentment for this situation.

Whether my husband chose to take advantage of this opportunity to get rid of his anger and resentment was going to be up to him. Whether he chose to see that a relationship is more important than anger was also up to him. But thankfully, the opportunity was seized and the outcome for my husband was successful. Although a small reluctance to forgive was present, my husband's anger, hostility, and resentment were turned into gentle understanding and compassion through reluctant forgiveness. For this I am grateful and overjoyed.

The opportunity for mediation with my business partner was definitely productive and uplifting. I am not going into great detail because our experience was very personal and very touching. This moment will remain cherished and just between the two of us. But I will say that we exchanged heartfelt apologies with tears and hugs, forgiveness was granted with smiles and laughter, and now the excitement of a fresh start begins for both of us.

Originally, the foundation of *my* pain was that I had felt deserted when I needed my business partner the most. He validated that pain and authentically apologized, which made forgiveness easy to grant. In return, I apologized for hurting him and his family, and he granted me his forgiveness. I have now withdrawn the legal action.

The act of forgiveness is one action, one unconditional loving action, to clean the slate, start fresh—a loving action of *undoing*. Through forgiveness, the negative destructive energy disappears. *You* don't clear the energy. The act of forgiveness through our Divine Source clears the energy. In the moment between my business partner, me, and our Divine Source, the slate was cleared and a fresh start began. That is forgiveness … that is a relationship!

* * *

CHAPTER THREE

Celebrating Spiritual Consciousness

However many holy words you read, however many you speak,
what good will they do you,
if you do not act upon them?

~The Buddha

A large portion of *The Shift* in Part Two was devoted to learning *how to recognize ego*. Why was that? For one reason only: to benefit *all* relationships. A great deal of effort and practice was spent dissecting the markings of ego and its pain. The pain that we feel is very real and very hurtful. So I thought I would now spend a little time on recognizing the *spiritual vibrational energy* within others.

During my NDE recovery, one of the most fearful things I had to overcome was *energy*; the *energy* of people. I didn't understand that when someone's outside energy was hostile, angry, or sad, I had the *ability* to sense their *inside energy*, which was soft, warm, and loving. The incongruity of these two energies sent horribly confusing messages, which often triggered my feelings of *not being normal*. Sensing the inside *spiritual vibrational energy* was not an ability I had before my near-death experience or before learning *spiritual consciousness*!

When I first saw my business partner at the courthouse, on the outside he was friendly, cordial, professional, and kind. But his inside energy was so fragile, soft, low, and quiet. It was almost like the feeling you get when you hear the scared, panicked cry of a small lost child in a mall; you want to pick him up, hug him, and reassure him that it will all be okay. When I felt this *inside energy* from my business partner, it broke my heart. The realization that I was the cause of this made me feel even more devastated.

Inside energy, or *spiritual vibrational energy*, is not of words, which is so difficult for me to explain. It's more like *sensing* or intuitively *knowing*. But this *gift* didn't come to me *because* of my NDE. This ability came to me through recognizing *spiritual consciousness*. So if I can do it, so can you! My near-death experience showed me positively that a *spiritual vibrational energy* exists within everyone, lives on forever, and is *that* part that allows us to communicate with spirit. My near-death experience showed me that *alert consciousness* is real.

So how do I teach you *how* to see the *spiritual vibrational energy* of others? Well, do you recognize *your own* ego? Do you see the ego of others? Do you recognize the difference between the man and his actions, and then do you love him anyway? Do you love and not *try* to love? Do you know the difference between *giving* and *trying*? Do you authentically forgive and totally forget? Do you apologize when you have done wrong? Do you know what forgiveness is? Do you wait to receive forgiveness even if it takes your entire lifetime? Do you see all of your brothers as no better or no worse than yourself? Can you feel Oneness? Let me ask you this: Do you *want* to *feel* the *spiritual vibrational energy* of others?

If you answered *no* to any one of these questions then you have some work to do. If you answered *yes* to all of these questions then you *can* feel the *spiritual vibrational energy* within others. If you can't hear it, then you are too focused on recognizing ego, which only feeds it.

There is no way to teach you to *see spiritual energy* or to *feel spiritual consciousness*; and do you know why? Your ego won't let me teach you. Only *you* can unlock your ego, know *love*, know *forgiveness*, know *giving*, and know *your brother*. It is through Oneness and recognizing that we *can* recognize ego's triggers that we are given *spiritual consciousness*.

If you have felt one trigger and recognized it; if you have validated and recognized that it was ego's pain; if you lived in the moment just once and if you felt authentic love and forgiveness just once, then I have done my job. And for this, I thank you for *trying*. Having you *try* is *all* that I hoped for, so thank you. From the moment you started reading, I have shared my painful journey of discovering *spiritual consciousness*. It is through my pain and discovery that you have felt what I mean. It is *feeling as I felt, being as I feel,* that has taught you what you have always known, but have merely forgotten.

The journey in finding *spiritual consciousness* and feeling *spiritual vibrational energies* doesn't have to be hard or take a long time; ego makes it so. The journey is your choice and fully in your control. It took me more than nine months to figure this out, and with this came a whole lot of pain and suffering. But it's your journey ... it's your choice to continue on.

Let me be clear: We are enjoying a human experience as *spiritual beings.* This means that the journey you are on is not to be rushed—it's a journey of re-discovering the relationship with your Divine Source, yourself, Oneness, and other higher *spiritual vibrational energies.* Our journey never ends. You *will* find *spiritual consciousness*, and when you do, the journey *will* continue as you *work* to keep it. When our *physical* journey ends and we transition to spirit, our *spiritual* journey continues.

It is *only* in recognizing ego within yourself and others that *alert consciousness* is found. It takes a whole lot of triggers, a little bit of pain, and a lot of patience and determination. But then, in an unexplainable instant, *spiritual consciousness* appears, waiting perfectly for you! I am no better or worse, and if I can do it so can you. But *do you want* to?

I wanted desperately to learn so I could stop my pain. I'm glad I did and that is why I am here today. I still have a lifetime of lessons to learn and many triggers to feel, but I am enjoying learning them in *spiritual consciousness*. Life is a whole lot easier. I am enjoying every minute of this journey, and I cherish every minute I am still on earth.

Our time on earth is precious and very fragile. Obviously we hope and plan for a long and healthy life, but our demise remains a mystery. During our lifetime we get to decide *how* we are going to spend it. We are either going to live in *alert consciousness* or *mindless consciousness* or a combination of the two. No matter what you decide to do, the actions you decide to take are perfectly fine. This last leg of our journey is not in judgment, and there are no right or wrong answers. This is merely an opportunity to wrap up everything we have learned together thus far, and to tantalize your curiosity before you leave *my classroom*.

Rest assured that whatever you have learned (remembered) up to this point will *never* leave you; you won't let it! You may forget some stuff, but in your journey of *spiritual consciousness* you are well on your way. Our physical human existence on earth is only about creating and growing relationships. Our spiritual existence on earth is about attaining *spiritual consciousness*.

There are four factors that assist us with our existence as we create and grow relationships and strive to attain *spiritual consciousness*. They are time, love, forgiveness, and ego.

Time is precious and unpredictable, and this can be frightening, as it was for me. The fear is felt because you are not using your allotted time wisely; you are wasting it. You do not waste time if you live in *alert consciousness*, and thus your fear of the unpredictability of life will vanish. Time is the foundation in relationships. If you don't give it enough time the relationship will fail, and if you give it too much it will drown. The purpose of time is to learn.

Ego is a tool created by our Divine Source, developed by us and used in our love relationships. This tool of ego causes triggers, which allow us the opportunity to see love, peace, and forgiveness. It's in *mindless consciousness* that we are triggered, but within *alert consciousness* we recognize everything. No matter what we decide to do with our triggers, the tool of ego continues to challenge our relationships so we may always have the opportunity to love and forgive.

In denying a trigger of ego you deny the lesson. In denying the lesson, you deny yourself the opportunity for a relationship with your Divine Source, with yourself, and with Oneness. Ego represents an opportunity to choose. It doesn't matter what action you choose; the only thing that matters is that you had a choice. The purpose of our ego is opportunity—opportunity to feel love, peace, and forgiveness, and the opportunity to choose.

Love is *anything* created by our Divine Source, all-knowing and all-loving. We are an extension of our Divine Source sharing all, created in Oneness. It is a state within our *spiritual consciousness,* connected to our Creator, where we are *being* and *doing* in a state of love for ourselves and others. The difference between love and happiness is that love is in *alert consciousness* and is ever-present in our relationships. Happiness is what we *mistake* for love in *mindless consciousness* and can fluctuate like triggers. Any action of love needs no justification; it is innocent and without expectation of gain. The most challenging love relationship we experience is that with ourselves. If you don't love yourself, how do you love others?

If we could truly see that we are all an extension of our Divine Source and connected to Oneness, how could we hurt any of our brothers? It's because of our connection to Oneness that we need to realize that when you harm or mistreat yourself or hurt another, you are harming our Oneness and Divine Source. This is not love. The purpose of love is *knowing.*

Forgiveness is a gesture of love. Forgiveness rights the wrongs, balances relationships, and is at the core of our *spiritual vibrational energy*. As extensions of our Divine Source, we all have the ability to forgive. The act of forgiveness is an unconditional, loving action that enables us to clean the slate and start fresh.

Forgiveness is only one action; it is a loving action of *undoing* within a relationship. The *undoing* is the clearing of negative and destructive energy. Humans forgive. Our Divine Source clears. It is our act of forgiveness through love that our Divine Source clears with love. The purpose of our forgiveness is *peace*.

Where there is forgiveness there will *not* be war. Eternity is found in relationships. It is the love and forgiveness we can show ourselves and our devotion to the Divine Source. In this physical, human existence, we have a limited amount of time and we never know *when* this time is up. In this time, we are either growing or dying, we are not doing both; we either are building or breaking; awake or sleeping; in *mindless consciousness* or *alert consciousness*. What do you choose?

* * *

CHAPTER FOUR

Heaven Time or Earth Time

Never leave that till tomorrow
which you can do today.

~Benjamin Franklin

For me there are two types of time: Earth time and Heaven time. First I am going to describe each one and then I am going to share with you the importance of time and what we should be doing with it.

Everyone seems to be on a great quest for happiness. Some are searching for financial freedom, peace and quiet, or their one true love.

Listen closely to what others are saying: *I will be happy when I find my soul mate*, or *when I have more money* or *when I have more spare time* or *when tomorrow's meeting is over....* The truth of the matter is, tomorrow really doesn't exist, yesterday really doesn't matter, and today is only a *perception of your reality*. All we really have is this minute ... that's it!

What is Earth time? Before my NDE I had nothing to compare time to. So what I knew of time is the same as what you know: sixty seconds makes a minute, sixty minutes is an hour, twenty-four hours in a day, and seven days comprise a week. Another thing: some of my days were so busy that there weren't enough hours in that day to get all my work done!

For me now, Earth time is so very precious. I think carefully about how I spend it and with whom I choose to spend it. I don't know *when* my clock is going to stop ticking, but I am *guaranteed* that someday it *will* stop. So no matter what I decide to do, my goal will be to have left this Earth a little better than I found it.

What is Heaven time? Heaven time has no seconds, minutes, hours, or days. It stands perfectly still, quiet, peaceful. There are no worries, to-do lists, schedules, or thoughts of wasting it. Why is Heaven time so different? There is no perception of *time* as with Earth time. Heaven time has no ego or perception, and therefore has no worry, pain, fear, or sadness.

Why is time so important? The Earth time we have presents an opportunity to learn. When we were born, I think we were each given a specific number of seconds in our lifetime to learn our lessons. We were *not* told how many seconds, but we are told to make the best use of them. Time is something that can't be bought, borrowed, or stolen. Through death, time can be taken without your permission and you can't do anything about it. Your time is a precious commodity that *you* allow others to waste, that *you* waste. If you knew that you had only 86,400 seconds left, what would you do with them?

Can Heaven time exist on Earth? Yes, it can and it does! Millions of people enjoy Heaven time every day. Heaven time doesn't exist in only blissful situations. Heaven time is living the moment—and there are some enjoying Heaven time right now. Do you know who they are? It was President Obama when his troops stormed Osama Bin Laden's compound. It is the children starving to death in Africa; it was the person buried alive in 9/11; and, it's a mother waiting for an ambulance for her daughter who is clinging to life after a car accident. It is also a man about to see his child being born; it is expectant grandparents about to meet their first grandchild. It is a mother feeding her newborn for the first time; and, it is when an unconscious father awakens days before his death to tell you he loves you and that everything will be okay. This is Heaven time. It is at your disposal, but the choice is yours. Do you want to live in Heaven time or Earth time?

When you live in Heaven time, you prioritize everything differently. You don't worry, you have faith, and there is a peaceful acceptance that you are not in control of this very moment. Heaven time is about feeling so small in the vast amount of Oneness, yet feeling so comforted and protected. Let's look at some everyday situations that we can recognize and where we can practice experiencing Heaven time.

The next time you are stuck in traffic or in a shopping lineup, watch what *other people* are doing with *their* Earth time; it's incredible! There is anger, agitation, frustration, hostility, and resentment. There is no peace or happiness. Heaven time is a blessing; it is an opportunity to exercise *the now* ... the moment ... the second ... a lesson in choice. So do you want Earth time or Heaven time? You choose.

Here's another example: when you are triggered by someone or a situation, are you going to chose Heaven time or Earth time? Earth time exists in ego and triggers; Heaven time is in the moment filled with clarity and love. You get to choose, it's your journey.

Lastly, another example is enjoying the company of someone you love. Let's take the precious moment with my dad in hospice, as an example. That was the last moment of my dad's life that I got to share with him. The moments are not going to be long and not always filled with pain. Spending that moment with him is what I will always remember and treasure, because it was in that moment that I was loved and felt peace and incredible joy.

When you are with someone you love, just stop for a moment and really feel that wonderful second and be immersed in gratitude that you are able to feel it; many don't. It could be while you are watching TV, enjoying a beautiful meal, sitting on a deck, laughing over something silly, enjoying a glass of wine, the moment you kiss one another goodnight or pass by them and pat them on the bum. Heaven time isn't just in hostile, sad, dire situations. Heaven time is all around us. But, most importantly, it is in Heaven time that we are connected to our Divine Source and enjoy the bounty of love and unfathomable wisdom. That is *Heaven Time*, and it is all yours. Just decide.

When you are in Heaven time, you choose what is important and what isn't. Again, our time on this physical plane is like the sand in an hourglass, except you can't see the sand, so you have no idea *when* it is going to run out. But, if you *did know* when your sand would run out, would you live life differently? How would you spend your money? Would you love differently? How would you give to others? How would you treat yourself? Would you keep the same job? Would you stay in the same relationships? *Now* what does your life look like?

Heaven time and Earth time correspond to living in *alert consciousness* or *mindless consciousness*. *Now* that we can appreciate the preciousness of time, what are we supposed to do with it? The purpose in understanding time is to enable you to choose to prioritize your thoughts and actions differently. It is in living in the moment, in *alert consciousness*, that you can recognize ego and receive messages of profound wisdom from higher *vibrational spiritual energies*. In *alert consciousness*, relationships grow and flourish and life is much easier to enjoy. The purpose of *mindless consciousness* is to *remind* us when we are *not* in *alert consciousness*! That's it!

Basically, my *Heaven Time* is a group of lessons *reminding* you of *all* that you *know*, and *some* of what you have *forgotten*. It's a reminder that our Earth clock is ticking and *this moment* could be *all* you have ... so make the most of what you've got. How *will* you spend your moment?

The remaining chapters will be spent on questions that so many people ponder; so much of our *clock time* is consumed with *why*. Are ghosts real? Why? Are there such things as angels? Why? Do haunted houses exist? Why? Are there really evil spirits? Why? ... And so much more.

In the next couple of final chapters, I will give you *my opinion* as to why we are so inquisitive, why we continue to search, and why we can't seem to quench our insatiable curiosity. Then I am going to give you *all* the *explanations* for some of your *questions*. I {my Choir} will share with you ... *why*!

* * *

CHAPTER FIVE

Angels, Ghosts, and Spirits

Angels are spirits, but it is not because they are spirits that they are angels.
They become angels when they are sent.
For the name angel refers to their office, not their nature.
You ask the name of this nature, it is spirit;
You ask its office, it is that of an Angel, which is a messenger.

~St. Augustine

Throughout my writing I emphasized that we are *Oneness*. It is only here and now that you will be able to come full circle and *truly* understand **Oneness**. Until you understood the beginning, you won't understand the end. This is the first time in the entire book that you have received the definition for Oneness. Now let me explain.

Oneness is {*the connectivity of the source of oneness physical and non-physical, spirit and non-spirit*}

I know it seems like a mouthful, so here is my best attempt at a translation:

ONENESS: The connectivity {*the actions of connecting; the activity of connecting; methods of coming together; One into/unto them all; All into/unto the One*} **of the Source of Oneness** {*the source from which all share; collectively equal and a part of; sharing equal and part of One*} **physical**

and non-physical, spirit and non-spirit.

In plain English, it means any actions, activities, and any method of coming together from one universal Source that is One unto all and the all unto It, no matter if it is physical or non-physical, spirit or non-spirit. Spirit is anything physically dead or spiritually alive.

So basically, dead or alive, human or animal, we are *all* connected and we *know* that *we are* connected ... but we *forget* until *reminded*. Our pets have a *spiritual energy*, and when they die, do *they* not continue to live on? Yes, of course they do. Their *true essence* of *what* they were, perceived by our five human senses, *will still* be able to *recognize* our pet's energy. Therefore, Oneness connects us to the universe: dead or alive, past or present; whether we remember it or not. Energy is energy.

We are first a *spiritual being* directly connected to the unfathomable wisdom of higher *vibrational spiritual energies*. Then we are a physical body with the ability to hear, see, feel, and communicate with higher vibrational energies. It is in understanding our fears of the *abnormal* that our recognition and acceptance will take fear's place by learning *alert consciousness*. Once *alert consciousness* is developed, our *spiritual consciousness* will allow us to celebrate such gifts as angels, ghosts, and spirit guides. Our curiosity will be satisfied because the ineffable wisdom from higher spiritual energies will automatically share *all* that we've forgotten.

It is my opinion that everyone has such an insatiable curiosity about the spirit world because they are trying to remember something they *unknowingly* forgot. *Oneness* keeps knocking on your door of curiosity, hoping that one day, you will figure out *how* to open the door. Please don't stop being curious; just learn *how* to open the door! That is why we are so curious, why we continually search, and why we can't seem to quench our insatiable curiosity. We are so focused on being curious we can't see the door and certainly have *forgotten* how to open it!

As we near the end, I will take this opportunity to share *my personal point of view* {Choir} on things that pique the curiosity of so many, such as angels, ghosts, spirit guides, reincarnation, etc. It is my hope that those who are fearful will no longer be so, and those who are curious will be somewhat satisfied. And for those who despair that *all* is lost, let hope inspire them.

Again, let's recap quickly for the last time. The most important part to our human being is our *spiritual vibrational energy*. This s*piritual vibrational energy* remains after the body is gone and, just as each person is an individual, so too is their *spiritual vibrational energy*. When the body transitions to death, it becomes a **spiritual vibrational energy**. *Spiritual* is not of physical form—it is invisible and created by a Higher Power; *vibrational* means that we can *all* feel it equally and its strength is capable of being raised or lowered; *energy* means an extension of all that comes from our Divine Source, such as the wisdom, love, and Oneness.

The night of my NDE, when I was with my dad, my *spiritual vibrational energy* felt so light, effortless, yet powerfully energized, all-knowing, capable of such easy communication. There were no negative feelings as we know here, only unconditional love, joy, happiness, peace, tranquility, perfectness. With all my heart, I wish that I could *magically zap* you and give you a sense of this peace so we could share the sense of freedom I felt. Please believe me when I say there isn't anything negative—only tranquil peace and unconditional love with blissful joy—just perfectness.

I believe that after our physical body transitions to death, there remains a high *spiritual vibrational energy*, which still attempts to communicate. The spirit world communicates at a very high vibrational level, difficult to hear for the untrained human body. If someone close to us dies, we are left to transition from grief. It is in our grief that we live in the moment more often, unknowingly in *alert consciousness*. It is then that our vibrational level is drastically increased and we can feel our deceased loved one around us. This presence is of love, kindness, reassurance, peace ... then our thinking, yappy-mind of ego, *mindless consciousness*, kicks in and says, "You're crazy, this can't be real, it must be your imagination."

When we live in *spiritual consciousness*, our *spiritual vibrational energy* level dramatically increases, allowing us to hear higher vibrational messages from spirit. While we are in human form I don't think we will ever be able to increase our spiritual vibrational level to *equal* that of spirit, but we can raise it high enough to hear, feel, and communicate. There are many who have mastered the ability to increase their *spiritual vibrational energy* level and are capable of communicating with the spirit world. We call them *gifted*, but what they really are is *talented*. *Gifted* implies that only a few possess the *ability*; we *all* possess the *ability* but few work hard at mastering it. The nature of Oneness states that those with *talent* are our equals, connected to the same Divine Source. We all possess the same abilities and opportunities; we all just choose differently.

As our physical body today communicates with a mouth, voice box, tongue, and physical body language, the *spiritual vibrational energy* of the deceased obviously cannot. So how *do* you *want it* to *communicate* with us? *Spiritual vibrational energy* is not aggressive, mean, hostile, or out to do you harm. The spirit world wants to communicate. However, without a body it is *difficult* for them *to send* you a message and have *you receive* it *accurately*.

Spiritual vibrational energy is *not* angry. It is unconditional love, the most tranquil peace, wisdom beyond human comprehension, fluid-like communication, and blissful joy. It is within *our perception* of yappy *mindless consciousness* that we think otherwise and create the negativity in our ego-mind. It is the lack of knowledge and understanding that keeps our fears alive and very real. Trust me!

The Bible is an accepted book of truth. Therefore, because angels and guardian angels are mentioned in the Bible, it is automatically accepted that they must be true, and there doesn't seem to be much controversy. Conversely, ghosts and spirit guides seem to fall within the realm of the paranormal, and in my view this is based in ignorance and fear. If it is not an angel filled with white light then the fear is that it's the opposite, the devil or negative energy. This is why the concept of *spiritual vibrational energy* is widely controversial—because it is based on perception. We all know by now that perception is ego and is capable of false truths and based in fear to cause pain. This is why the *paranormal* is a topic for many fundamental debates and arguments. Basically, it is a topic where ego clashes with other egos.

To be clear: This chapter was written solely to share my personal view with you, based on my experience, growth, and recovery. I am writing within *spiritual consciousness*, not to provoke fear or clash with ego. If I trigger something within you that you don't agree with or don't like ... then you're welcome! Consider that trigger a gift from me. I am not trying to convince anyone of anything, nor am I looking to debate these topics. My purpose is to share, not to aggravate.

Angels

I believe that angels exist and assist us every day. Angels are the humans that have transitioned to spirit; they have acquired an unimaginable level of wisdom to be shared with man. Angels appreciate our human existence, with its struggles and pain; they have lower vibrational levels so they may be heard more easily. Their communication is like a go-between us and those even higher vibrational levels that haven't walked in man's suffering shoes. Their purpose is to understand, educate, and communicate. It seems that angels translate to and with other energies whose vibrational levels are too high for direct communication with our lower human vibrational levels.

Guardian Angels

Guardian angels are "graduated" angels set out to guide *you* specifically. As you grow and develop, so do guardian angels. Depending on the moment in time, you may have more than one, possibly many. They may not always be the same; they may change as you grow and develop. Their vibrational level appears higher and a little harder to hear at all times.

Spirit Guides

These guides may have the lowest vibrational level and are therefore much easier to hear and feel. They are very patient and are knowledgeable; they feel as if they understand our existence. They are always around, guiding and helping. It feels as if we know of them or should know *of* them.

Ghosts

The word *ghost* is like the word *death*. People think that death is *a place to go* rather than the *transition* to something else. When I think of the word *ghost*, I'm not thinking of a person or entity but rather a *way of communication*. The clichéd notion of a ghost is that it's an apparition, something to view. So let's not confuse what we *feel* and *know* with what we *see*. A ghost is another way of communication; it is not an entity but energy's communication mode.

Negative Energies

From my experience, and now through further spiritual growth, I feel that negative energies are a form of communication. If a message is not being received, the *vibrational spiritual energy* will start to make itself heard. If you don't hear that, the message will get louder. Your perception of this energy could be that of negativity. Within *spiritual consciousness* I do not feel negativity. I am not saying for one minute that negative energies do not exist. All I am saying is that they don't exist within *spiritual consciousness*; they exist within ego's perception.

Paranormal

Paranormal, as a label, is the whole wastebasket that contains everything for which we do not have any logical answer. It was a huge stigma for me. I dislike the word *paranormal* because it made *me* feel not-normal. However, paranormal is just that: what science can't prove, what religion doesn't like, and what ego needs to label. Here comes paranormal!

Paranormal is a generic concept. Say you didn't like to eat potatoes; you wouldn't then say that you don't like food! You would say that it is the food called potatoes you don't care for. But you wouldn't try to convince someone that a potato isn't food, would you? Well, that is why I have such an aversion to the word "paranormal." Everything within the spirit world *is* normal; everything in ego is *not* normal. Everything *paranormal* is *not* misunderstood. It is just a blanket of a word that instigates fear, stimulates curiosity, perpetuates lack of knowledge, and creates pain.

Although I have come a long way in my own personal journey, I continue to learn and grow in *spiritual consciousness*. The fact that you live in *spiritual consciousness* doesn't mean you *have* all the answers, but it does mean that you know *where* to get the answers! My *spiritual consciousness* expands each day as I question many of life's mysteries and *plain old* curiosities. As I have shared my journey and my spiritual consciousness, I will now share answers to some of the questions that I've been asked, hopefully quenching some of your curiosity too.

* * *

CHAPTER SIX

Answers to Your Questions

Make friends with the angels, who though invisible are always with you....
Often invoke them, constantly praise them, and make good use of their help
and assistance in all your temporal and spiritual affairs.

~St. Francis De Sales
Introduction to the Devout Life

*S*ince living in spiritual consciousness, I too have pondered many of life's mysteries and the meaning of our existence. Where is God when we have natural disasters? Do we have more than one soul mate? Is there more than one level in the afterlife? Are there really such things as guardian angels and archangels? Do murderers go to Heaven?

Being in spiritual consciousness, I was able to learn lessons and receive profound answers to not only my questions, but other people's questions as well. This wisdom came to me in the form of heavenly spiritual teachers that I have called my Choir. I have received incredible answers to many of my controversial questions and gained insightful knowledge about the challenges we face today in our fractured existence.

If you are curious and want to know the *spirit world's view* on karma, suicide, ghosts, and the end of the world, etc., here it is. Please remember that what you are about to read is opinion only. The translation of my Choir that I share is not intended to instigate fear or debate, but merely to attempt to satisfy the curiosity that already exists. It may sound choppy or be grammatically incorrect, so please read for content and message. Some of the topics seem to overlap one another and, for that reason, they have been grouped together.

Conception-Abortion-Miscarriages?

Choir: *{In Oneness we all belong; a human being is Divine Source's creation; created with the ability to reproduce; the creation is the union that duplicates human being; Divine Source gifts spiritual vibrational energy. Therefore each conception contains spiritual vibrational energy. Miscarriages contain spiritual vibrational energy and will be reunited upon transition. Miscarriages are unfulfilled human form. Unfulfilled human form with spiritual vibrational energy, are errors ... man, environment. Human reproduction is of man, man is capable of errors; Divine Source-spiritual energy is not. Spiritual vibrational energy that Divine Source gifts and that human form cannot be fulfilled, still remains with Oneness and reunited upon transition. Abortion is planned miscarriage, still with spiritual vibrational energy, still part of Oneness, still without human form and decision of man. There is no judgment, only love.}*

Lorri: As man can chose to procreate he can also choose to terminate. No matter what man's choice is, at conception the gift of *spiritual vibrational energy* is present. The *spiritual vibrational energy* of the unfulfilled human's form resulting in abortion or miscarriage goes back to Oneness. Humans make mistakes, errors; the Divine Source does not. Humans can be judgmental; Divine Source is not.

Marriage—Divorce—Soul mates?

Choir: *{Marriage is of man, civil law, rules. The union of man is divine. The relationship, coming together Oneness, union, love, forgiveness, is divine. Divorce is man, rules, law, matters* (like business) *not of union or* *relationship. Soul mates more than one; human existence is union of relationship, Oneness. No limitations in Oneness; no judgment with non-matters of union, the union of Oneness is what is celebrated.}*

Lorri: What we call a "soul mate" doesn't seem to register with my Choir. "Matter" is like the business or laws of man and doesn't seem to register either. Basically, the union (relationship) of man is a divine union of Oneness filled with love and forgiveness. There are no limitations in Oneness; if your *soul mate* dies there is another one for you—if you choose. Oneness is about union of relationships, love and forgiveness. It's not about divorce or staying widowed out of loyalty; that concept doesn't seem to register with them. Resisting showing love to another human being is not the nature of Oneness; therefore it doesn't seem to register with them.

Karma—Coincidences—Consequences?

Choir: *{Human form and spiritual vibrational energy in Oneness has purpose, no coincidence. Oneness is purposeful interconnectivity. Consequence is purposeful error of man ... error isn't "bad or good," error is outcome. Man purposes consequence then tries to escape accountability blaming it on Oneness. Karma is Oneness. Karma is a knocking door, open it and learn, turn deaf to it, it will still keep knocking, turn blind to it, it will still keep knocking. Once door to Karma is open, manifestation begins.}*

Lorri: There are no coincidences in life because Oneness is purposefully interconnected. Now a consequence is the outcome of human action. Karma is manifestation in Oneness, ask and you will receive. Careful what you ask for!

Suicide—Reincarnation?

Choir: *{Spiritual vibrational energy and human form; no different than abortion or miscarriage, error of man; error not necessarily bad or good, matter (business) of man. No judgment on decision, only love and forgiveness. Human form needs not to justify. All spiritual vibrational energy transitioned* *from form to spirit will reunite with Oneness that is how it is meant to be. Reincarnation is spiritual vibrational energy without human form, not reusable, one energy one form; form eliminated ... still, the same, one energy.}*

Lorri: To commit suicide is the choice of we humans, similar to that of abortion. Divine Source is only love and forgiveness and doesn't judge or condemn the business or the decision of human. Whether its abortion, miscarriage, accidental death, or suicide, all spiritual vibrational energies that transition from form to spirit will be reunited with Oneness. They will be reunited with the Divine Source.

Reincarnation feels like a *spiritual vibrational energy* imprint. It feels like it was a single vibrational energy that was once a form. It continually resurfaces to allow us to sense their imprint of what was once here. Almost like a déjà vu, except for someone else's life!

Hell—Devil—Sin?

Choir: *{Spiritual vibrational energy is of Oneness, extended from Divine Source; errors of man and matters of man are Hell and sin. Sin is nothing more than error of man ... like a mistake. Mistakes are easily forgiven and quickly corrected; all mistakes are equal. Man has different perception, makes sin greater than mistake, and is not all equal. Although equal to mistake, man makes sin and the act of doing, punishable with a burden of a possible non-qualification for forgiveness. Sin is unrecognizable to Divine Source, man created perception of sin and the burden of sin. Hell is matters of man, varying acts of qualification to go to a place of ill. Who decides what qualifies? Is not then, any mistake, qualification to go? Upon transition, Divine Source reclaims the spiritual vibrational energy to live forever.}*

Lorri: We are all spiritual vibrational energies created by the Divine Source and we all celebrate the nature of Oneness; whether you know it or not. The difference between a mistake and a sin is the varying degrees of severity based in human perception. What the Choir is saying is that human error is human error. As humans we are going to err; that is how we learn.

When we transition from human form to spirit, the Divine Source reclaims your *spiritual vibrational energy* to live forever. In reclaiming, there will be a life review, *your* life review of all errors and all your goodness positioned in Oneness. So do murderers go to Heaven? Yes, but not until Divine Source reclaims their *spiritual vibrational energy*.

Forgiveness—Repenting?

Choir: *{Spiritual vibrational energy is an extension of Divine Source participating in Oneness. Human form is capable of mistakes, also capable of wisdom, love, and forgiveness. Upon transition, all mistakes of human form will be corrected and eliminated. Spiritual Energy cannot be destroyed, No mistakes or errors destroys spiritual vibrational energy, which is a gift of Divine Source and will remain a gift long after the human form is gone. That gift of spiritual vibrational energy is always perfect, perfectly loving, forgiving, wise ... it is human form that is not. Upon the death of human form, so too is death of its errors and mistakes; any essence of the spiritual vibrational energy will be gifted back to Divine Source from where it first came.}*

Lorri: Spiritual vibrational energy cannot be destroyed. As we exist in human form we make mistakes-errors to teach us and bring us closer to Oneness. Upon transition and after the Divine Source reclaims our *spiritual vibrational energy*, all mistakes of human form will be corrected and eliminated. But we don't have to wait for death to receive forgiveness. You have forgiveness right before you each day. You have the choice to be actively and consciously a part of Oneness directly connected to Divine Source. Even if you don't, either way is fine because any essence of your *spiritual vibrational energy* will be gifted back to Divine Source from where it first came.

Faith—Hope—Belief?

Choir: *{Faith, hope, and belief are of human form. They are all of perception. Neither is better or worse but the same. The only difference is belief changes with knowledge, hope changes with pain of errors, and faith is like* *a gauge fluctuating as the human is connecting with their spiritual vibrational energy. Upon feeling their spiritual vibrational energy level the faith then behaves like a knowing. All three do not survive the transition of death. The spiritual vibrational energy knows and doesn't require faith, it is perfectly knowing.}*

Lorri: I will honestly admit that just after my near-death experience this was the hardest for me. I had no hope, only weak, questioning faith and I absolutely did not believe that this could even be logically possible. This was the hardest part of my recovery: faith, hope and belief. Even today as this manuscript is slowly transitioning into a book, I allow doubt and fear to creep into my thoughts, weakening my hope and belief that readers will enjoy my message. Then my faith—spiritual consciousness—thank goodness, kicks ego's butt! I am no different than you, with the same sort of questions, doubts and insecurities.

Manifestation?

Choir: *{Manifestation is not faith, hope, or belief. It is aligning, asking, and automatically receiving. Manifestation is not a secret or special gift; it is in Oneness and created equally for all. There is no qualification process; ask and it is given. There is no right or wrong, manifestation is just what it is. To be given is to be heard, if not heard or heard incorrectly then what was heard will be given. You will be given exactly what you asked for. When you don't know when to ask or how to ask you will still be given what was heard. But if, what you eventually got was NOT what you asked for, the root is not what was given but the error in asking. Learn when and how to ask, and you will receive exactly what was requested ... that is manifestation.}*

Lorri: Manifestation is for everyone and it doesn't require any qualification. It's not a secret or special gift, but a way of communication. The most important part about manifesting is when to ask. First you must be aligned in *spiritual consciousness*, and then what you ask for will be from *alert consciousness* so it won't be influenced by ego. The problem is we try to manifest from yappy *mindless consciousness* with ego influence only to receive exactly what we asked for ... which isn't what we wanted!

Haunting—Ghosts?

Choir: *{Transitioned from human form that can be seen, felt, heard to spirit form of spiritual vibrational energy that can be still seen, felt, and heard, only different; form is gone but energy remains. This form of communication is registered differently by each. Spiritual vibrational energy has different levels. Communication goes each way, one with the other. If both vibrational levels are low, a lower energy will communicate; if only in high vibrational frequency, only high spiritual vibrational energies will communicate. As you can't find darkness in light, you can't find light in darkness; likes attract likes. As manifestation, you will communicate with that which your spiritual vibrational energy level is. Residual energy is Oneness, human questions not what is it, but why is it? ... answer is Oneness.}*

Lorri: When the physical form of a human transitions to energy that is what we can still feel. Energy is always in transition; sometimes it has a higher vibrational level. High vibrational levels have more strength, can be felt more and can do more. Some people will call this haunting or ghosts. But really it is just a simple form of communication. If your vibrational energy is particularly high then you might experience more activity than others. It is not meant to frighten you, but to communicate. Until I learned and understood more, this was a very frightening part of my recovery and I totally can empathize with anyone who may be frightened by this sort of energy. Please know that it is only *loud love* and not meant to intimidate or frighten. The sooner you embrace it, the sooner it will go away.

End of the World?

Choir: *{End of the world is fear, errors, mistakes. There is no such thing as end, only transition; end is perception; where there is perceived end there is only beginning. The greatest of man's fears is end of life. Death of the body* *is beginning of transition ... no end. End of an era, is but beginning of another ... no end, only transition. There can only be one end. That is the end of Fear. Fear has no transition. What could fear transition to ... only Peace!}*

Lorri: The phrase *"The End of the World"* can instigate and perpetuate such fear in so many people. If we truly believed that nothing ends, only transitions, then every time ego triggers your fear of *the end* realize that it's really the end of fear. Fear is the only thing that can end and it transitions to Peace. The end of the world ... is the *End of Fear* ... the *End of Ego* ... and isn't it about time?

* * *

Well, there you have it! Now let me share with you how this book was written and why you might have found some parts slower than others. The first part was written to reach your *mindless consciousness.* It was a compelling story, fast-paced, and filled with emotion.

The second part was written to tap into your *alert consciousness* so you could feel honest epiphanies without ego influence. The more honest you were with yourself the more epiphanies you might have experienced, the easier the transition. It might have felt like a slower read and much more difficult to get through. It might have seemed to lag and didn't get to the point fast enough for ego. As I said in the very beginning, first you are going to sit back and *feel* and then you are going to be *doing.* The first part uses your emotion—ego; the second part uses logic which is your mind—*alert consciousness.*

This is a *feel things out for yourself* book. If you got only one epiphany, felt *alert consciousness* for just one second, and recognized ego only one time, then I have done my job. Thank you for reading and joining me on this journey. You may need to re-read this book, gleaning a little more and more each time. I truly hope you enjoyed this experience and I wish you much love, peace, and patience in your spiritual journey.

* * *

GLOSSARY

Alert Consciousness: State of the mind that is directly connected to Divine Source; ability to communicate with high spiritual vibrational energy(s); able to live in the moment; able to recognize that you are recognizing; aware of misleading perceptions; able to make gentle corrections; acknowledges mind's flaws and accepts corrections.

Authentic purpose: Being as you were created; state of spiritual consciousness.

Awakening: Heightened level of spiritual intuitiveness.

Being: A form of physical or mental existence.

Beta blocker: A drug that slows down the heart and blocks substances like adrenaline when present in the system.

Choir: A representation of a collective group of highly vibrational spiritual energies that offers as one.

Connectivity: {the actions of connecting; the activity of connecting; methods of coming together; One into/unto them all; All into/unto the One}

Conscious Mind: A mindful state of being, doing, acting, and feeling while having the knowledge to separate a thought from a perception and knowing that you are doing it in that moment.

Death: Is *only* a process of transition, it is not *a place* to go but *how* you transition. It is a transition from *solid physical being* into a *vibrational spiritual being*.

Divine Source: One Supreme Being responsible for creation of Oneness.

Ego: {an energetic state of being we created within the yappy mindless consciousness which we developed out of pain; slowly losing our true sense of self by tuning out our alert consciousness, thereby disabling our spiritual consciousness making it impossible to hear or feel any messages being sent from our Divine Source}

Faith: A spiritual knowing.

Forgiveness: Is only one action; it is a loving action of *undoing* within a relationship; the *undoing* is the clearing of negative and destructive energy; humans forgive; Divine Source clears; it is *our* act of forgiveness through love that our Divine Source clears with love. The purpose of our forgiveness is peace.

Giving: {*doing without any thought about getting in return; giving is done without complaining during or after; giving is when you can, not when you think you should; giving is the act of love and done in your highest good; giving is innocent; giving is within the intention of your spiritual vibrational energy*}

Human Being: Created by One Divine Source; shares the same energy as Divine Source; shares Source of Oneness; created with two parts—the energy from Divine Source and physical form from man.

IANDS: International Association for Near-death Studies.

Mindless Consciousness: A state of the mind where perceptions, negativity, and mindless thoughts exist; a.k.a. yappy side of thinking; dysfunctional thought process without any recognition; opposite of alert consciousness; unable to be connected to your spiritual vibrational energy; cannot comprehend or sense any intuitiveness. Its purpose is to remind you when *not* in alert consciousness.

NDERF: Near-Death Experience Research Foundation.

Oneness: The connectivity of the Source of Oneness either physical or non-physical, spirit, or non-spirit. Any actions, activities, and any method of coming together from one universal Source that is One unto all and the all unto It, no matter if it is physical or non-physical, spirit or non-spirit. Spirit is anything physically dead or spiritually alive.

Pre–déjà vu: A snippet of a picture, related to a future event that hasn't physically shown itself, as of the current moment in time.

Process of Recognition: Trauma or conflict; Struggle with emotions; Search for Relief; Vibrational Shift; and then Peace or Resolution.

Recognizing: *Consciously recognizing* something, and then, *consciously acknowledging* that which you *already recognized.*

Residual Energy: Lingering energy from physical or spiritual form that can be felt, seen, smelled, heard, or touched; varying degrees of intensities having a positive or negative effect on others surrounding the lingering energy.

SVT: Supraventricular Tachycardia; Heart arrhythmia that needs immediate medical attention to convert back to normal rhythm.

Sensing: An unexplainable, intuitive *knowing;* done without intelligence, logic, thought, or reasoning.

Source of Oneness: Supreme greatness; source of equality; source of all wisdom, love, and knowledge; source of connectivity; almost beyond imagination or comprehension. *{the source from which all share; collectively equal and a part of; sharing equal and part of One}*

Spiritual Consciousness; Spiritually Conscious: Human state of mind which allows an experiencer heightened spiritual intuitiveness, heightened vibrational levels, acute psychic awareness, or profound state of higher consciousness or awakening; it is the feelings *of* the body, receiving messages *in* the mind, from higher spiritual vibrational energies.

Spiritual Enlightenment: Heightened level of spiritual intuitiveness or higher consciousness.

Spiritual Essence: Not physical or a dream; being in clarity; in the moment.

Spiritual Intuitiveness: Spiritual Consciousness.

Spiritual Vibrational Energy: Energy shared from Divine Source; a.k.a. spirit, soul, or spiritual energy; energy shared from Oneness; extension of, and always connected to, Divine Source and Oneness; an open line of communication; isn't capable of errors; allows mind to hear messages of wisdom; isn't capable of dying; energy remains after the body dies; its purpose is Divine communication.

Spiritual Vibrational Shift: An awareness in the conscious mind that causes a shift in *conscious knowing* when you are *recognizing* that you *recognized*. *{anything that causes or makes to cause a re-closeness, reuniting, reconnecting to the Divine Source from once you were}*

Trigger: A warning signal to pay attention, with your emotions acting as your gauge of seriousness.

Trying: is *{an intention to attempt willingly or unwillingly to perform an action knowing that failure is an acceptable option where the outcome may or may not be beneficial to me}*

Vibrational Energy: Intense energy that can be sensed; similar to intensity of a tuning fork or the heat from a bonfire.